C000089271

Foreign competition in Japan

Foreign competition in Japan

Human resource strategies

Robert J. Ballon

London and New York

First published 1992
by Routledge
11 New Fetter Lane, London EC4P 4EE

Simultaneously published in the USA and Canada
by Routledge
a division of Routledge, Chapman and Hall, Inc.
29 West 35th Street, New York, NY 10001

Typeset in Times Roman by Leaper & Gard Ltd, Bristol
Printed and bound in Great Britain by
Biddles Ltd, Guildford and King's Lynn

British Library Cataloguing in Publication Data
Ballon, Robert J. *1919–*
    Foreign competition in Japan : human resource strategies.
    1. Japan. Personnel. Management
    I. Title
    658.300952

    ISBN 0–415–06980–7

Library of Congress Cataloging in Publication Data
Ballon, Robert J.
        Foreign competition in Japan : human resource strategies / Robert
J. Ballon.
            p.   cm.
        Includes bibliographical references and index.
        ISBN 0–415–06980–7
        1. Corporations, Foreign—Japan—Personnel management.   I. Title.
HF5549.2.J3B35   1992
    658.3—dc20   91-2818
                                                                CIP

Contents

Tables

Figures

Preface

Both the theme and the author of this valuable book warrant special attention. The book is about Japan's employment system and the rather unusual way in which human resources are organized and motivated in the Japanese corporation. It is clear that the Japanese firm has succeeded to an unusual degree in constructively linking the interests of the organization and its members. It is clear too that this may well be the single most important competitive advantage of the Japanese company in international competition.

It is, however, a system of human resource utilization that poses special problems for the foreign company seeking to operate in Japan. Recruiting is difficult at all levels, and recruiting of experienced and really capable managers nearly impossible, for the foreign firm. Some companies with years of hard-won experience and success have managed to bridge the many gaps in values, perceptions and understanding. But for most foreign firms, issues of human resource management have become the most formidable barrier to effective Japan operations, far outweighing legal or administrative barriers.

This book is a thorough and timely review of the human resource management approach in Japan, with detailed presentations of critical and current data on the subject; it also deals knowledgeably with these issues as they affect the operations of foreign companies in Japan. The topic demands the attention of senior management of international companies, whether in Japan or not, for there is much to learn and apply to human resource management outside, as well as within, Japan.

The impact of the book is greatly heightened by the distinction of the author. Robert Ballon has played an extraordinary role in post-war Japan. He is a dedicated member of the faculty of Sophia University, and has performed with distinction both as educator and administrator in the move of that university to a leading position among Japan's private institutions of higher learning.

Professor Ballon, early in his four decades of study and work in Japan, realized the key role of human resource management in driving Japan's economic and social progress. He has been a pioneer in the analysis of human relations in Japanese industry, against the background of his broader efforts to understand and appreciate better what it is that makes Japan a special social organization – his continuing concern with 'Japaneseness'. His respect and affection for Japan's people informs and warms his book, and indeed all of Ballon Sensei's work.

His appreciation of the situation of the foreign firm in Japan derives not only from academic observation but from direct involvement in the issues of foreign company management as consultant and as organizer of a continuing series of seminars for foreign executives in Japan. Thus he can speak, as he does in this book, to the specific operational concerns of the foreign company. Not least, Professor Ballon brings to the subject the perspective of a European observer.

All too often, the reference for comparative analysis of Japan is to the United States, and the perspective of the analyst is that of a North American. Professor Ballon's European perspective is not only a useful counterbalance to the usual discussion, but is of particular value since Japan and the United States often present extremes in social and economic practice while European economies and societies are more often at a mid-point, making the comparisons less polar.

We are indebted to Robert Ballon for his long and sympathetic study of Japan, and for now providing this insightful analysis of Japan's human resource challenge, a summary of decades of research and experience.

James C. Abegglen

Introduction

'There is a strong consensus among [foreign] executives that global companies today must have a strong presence in Japan to remain viable long term competitors.' This statement appeared in a fairly recent study prepared for the American Chamber of Commerce in Japan and the Council of the European Business Community (1987), challenging the future of multinational corporations. Few doubt the attractiveness of Japan's market. But for many foreign businessmen, the *one* handicap of this market is the unfamiliar way in which the Japanese competitors and consumers operate, and this can be intimidating.

The qualification *Japanese* is perhaps misleading. Westerners usually use it in the same sense that American, French, or German is used. This implies a common denominator which is Western in origin and meaning. (Historians generally agree that the nation-state emerged in Europe after the Peace of Westphalia in 1648, at which time Japan as far as the Japanese were concerned had already had many centuries of continuous history.) *Japanese* in this sense is too Western a qualification. Much of what is described as *Japanese* is based on plain common sense, but common sense is not exactly viewed as a national characteristic. For example, the fact that a non-confrontational labour–management relationship makes good business sense is not peculiarly Japanese. Nor is the fact that Japanese individuals and institutions have a high regard for *learning by doing*, contrary to the Western way of downgrading it as learning the hard way.

Why would competing in Japan be the acid test of international business? Conducting operations in Japan is essential not only because of the opportunities offered in the Japanese market but also because of the challenge Japanese competitors have created in this market (not to mention in world markets). Competition in Japan's domestic market is fierce. Facing Japanese competitors in their home market is a must, for it is generally agreed that the international strength of Japanese companies is often built on their survival in their own market. A foreign firm that competes only as a vicarious presence through licensing or an import–distribution agreement is taking the least effective approach. For many years, presence through a joint venture was felt as a necessity imposed by the Japanese government; in more recent years, the majority of newly established subsidiaries are of the wholly owned type. These operations, with views ranging from Japan as a spot market to Japan as a component of global strategy, are essentially controlled by the home office. The problem is that the home office tends to rely mostly on quantitative and financial evidence and to assume that operations can to a considerable extent be handled by remote control. But the need is growing for a presence in Japan that goes beyond basic operations.

This means that Japan must be dealt with in Japanese terms, i.e. using the same dimensions that the Japanese themselves apply to the market and its institutions. The multinational corporation's global strategy must integrate a strategy specifically designed by (not *for*) Japan. Figures are helpful but they do not cover the full range of problems and expectations. The difference arises in the interpretation of these figures by the home office and by those in the Japanese subsidiary, both the local as well as foreign staff. The purpose of this corporate presence is to institutionalize time and space, the two fundamental dimensions shaping reality.

An unmistakably fundamental dimension of competing in Japan is to think long term; in other words, to have patience. An effective corporate image has to be established, i.e. the image not as projected by the home office and its expatriate representatives, but as viewed by the staff, suppliers, distributors and customers, all of whom are Japanese. Most products or services are fundamentally identical, but the image of the producer from the receiver's point of view is what determines a successful presence in the marketplace. Presence on the market is required to feel the cutting edge of Japanese competition. Patience is a requisite in accumulating experience painstakingly gathered over the years. This learning process needs to be institutionalized.

Japan, like any other country, has its idiosyncrasies, which was not a problem as long as they arose from origins understood as being exotic. Today not much that is exotic is left about the Japanese competitor. If unfamiliarity with Japanese practices (organization, personnel, marketing, etc.) can lead to disaster, the reason for such an outcome would be no different from the case of Western practices: simply that business activities reflect the values of the people performing them.

The challenge of competing in Japan may be summarized in two main propositions. First, what Western businessmen expect to control through economic ratiocination, the Japanese expect to achieve with interdependence of the people and institutions concerned. This leads to the second proposition: results expressed in figures are important but not as much as the process which manages people. The human-resource challenge of competing in Japan is to orchestrate an appropriate corporate presence based on the characteristics of Japan's labour market, Japan's workplace, and Japan's marketplace.

Each chapter of this book takes up one of these characteristics and concludes with a review of the policies and practices observed in foreign firms. The chapters are arranged in three parts as follows:

PART I THE LABOUR MARKET

Japanese society supports industry with human resources of outstanding quality (Chapter 1), and both society and industry work hand in hand at devising an effective employment system whereby human resources are hired more for their long-term potential than for their immediate contribution (Chapter 2). Hence the key importance of the work environment is stressed, since continuous training and development play a decisive role in labour–management relations, whether a labour union is involved or not, by supporting the concern for corporate survival (Chapter 3). Small in number, most foreign firms in Japan suffer from the major handicap of having very limited access to the general labour market. Consequently they become dependent on a special niche in the market where recruiting does not compare favourably with Japanese competitors.

PART II THE WORKPLACE

Japanese competitors place a great deal of value on the human resources they extract at considerable cost from the labour market, because employees are a long-term investment. Out of necessity, work compensation must be long-term, as indicated by the elaborate compensation system used (Chapter 4). The integration of human resources follows an organic style of corporate organization (Chapter 5), where the primary role of the manager is coordinator (Chapter 6) and not the exclusive and indispensable decision-maker (Chapter 7).

The way Japanese competitors retain their workforce is not by short-term management but by long-term development. Executives and managers of foreign firms, be they expatriate or Japanese, tend to be constrained by policies and practices that are often not of their own choosing and lacking in time perspective.

PART III   THE MARKETPLACE

The long-term characteristics of employment and how they affect the nature of the enterprise are factors shaping an aggressively competitive marketplace. But the Japanese competitor, namely his force of 'corporate members' (*sha-in*), does not expect to win the race all by himself; his success will depend on his capacity to marshal the support of all the participants in the market – suppliers, distributors, even users. In Japan, business transactions are rarely expressed through a legal contract; they conclude upon relationships where human considerations are predominant (Chapter 8). This is how competitive quality has become the key to market share, i.e. corporate survival (Chapter 9). Foreign firms have the appearance of neglecting the human dimension of Japan's marketplace. Competing in Japan requires the foreign firm to establish a sophisticated corporate presence, one resulting not so much from the sale of products or services but from the quality and experience of its human resources nurtured locally (Chapter 10). This may be a strategic consideration applicable to confronting the challenge of doing business in East Asia.

Our observations are based on a 30-year experience of organizing several hundreds of seminars for executives in the foreign firms, both expatriate and Japanese. Known as the International Management Development Seminars (IMDS), they are sponsored by Sophia University (Tokyo), promoting further the institution's international role in education. These seminars provide the foreign business community with a forum where opinions and experiences about doing business in Japan and with Japan can be exchanged and reviewed. When these seminars were first started few books describing Japanese business in English were available; today such books are abundant. The authors of several of them, in fact, were speakers at these seminars. Their knowledge and, more so, their *human* experiences are indispensable in undertaking the challenge of competing in Japan.

Heartfelt gratitude for many years of fruitful cooperation is expressed to Hideo Inohara and Yasuko Hamabata. For sprucing up the text of this volume sincerest thanks are extended to Linda Arakaki.

This volume is dedicated with respect and affection to my colleagues at Sophia University, both Japanese and non-Japanese alike, who as educators generously contribute time and energy to the task of exposing Japan to the world and the world to Japan. For over 40 years of my life in Japan they have made my environment a stimulating one, for which I am grateful.

R.J. Ballon

Part I
The labour market

Especially after World War II, Japanese society has been providing its industry with human resources of a high and uniform quality. The hallmark of this industry is an employment system whose norm is, but which is not always the case, stability; this means that employment is, whenever and wherever possible, a long-term consideration. The Japanese competitor hires employees not so much for their immediate use but for their potential in the long run. Training and development thus becomes vital to the work environment, a major responsibility of the company itself. In general, relations between management and the workforce have been conducive to a congenial corporate environment.

For such a thriving economy, the number of foreign firms, in any category, is surprisingly small. Employing 2 per cent of the labour force, they have established a narrow niche in the labour market, with little overall appeal. Although the individual foreign firm does not have much control over its situation, it contributes to its own dilemma by pursuing 'foreign' policies. Even when working conditions are comparable to those of Japanese competitors what is often missing is a work environment providing satisfaction commensurate with the expectations of the local workforce.

1 Society and economy

In terms of modernization and industrialization, what the West taught Japan and Japan adopted from the West is indeed impressive. From the recorded accounts of the twentieth century, the following events reveal the extent of Japanese progress:

- In the 1900s, Japan brought Western imperialism to a halt in East Asia by defeating Russia, which was then a Western power;
- In the 1920s, world trade, at the time largely dominated by Western nations, was challenged by Japanese products copied from Western products and sold at lower prices;
- In the 1940s, Japan terminated Western colonialism in its part of the world, albeit by attempting to impose its own brand of colonialism;
- In the 1960s, Western technological superiority was challenged by imported technology which was being improved to meet world market expectations;
- In the 1980s, by becoming the no. 1 creditor country in the world, Japan put an end to Western financial hegemony.

This is indeed a remarkable record for 'the first *non*-Western country to industrialize' based upon the Western model. It also represents a phenomenal transformation of Japan itself. Considering its progress, it may well be that Japan is developing some alternative model altogether. Surprisingly, its success was achieved by a country whose only abundant resource was people. Unlike other manifestations of modernization, as in clothing or hair-style, Japan did not respond to the development of its human resources by a mere imitation of the West. This was achieved by turning to its own dynamic values and practices.

HUMAN RESOURCES

Human resources affect economic performance not so much by the number of individuals and their individual qualities, but by the interaction of these individuals within the institutions they create. In the case of Japan two criteria are especially relevant, educational level and social dynamics.

Level of education

> Contemporary Japan is about as developed and organized a society as one can find today. It is a society of employers and employees, where educational credentials and educated skills are central to employment, promotion, and general social status. Japan is a meritocracy shaped by educational competition. And this is fitting, for Japan is a nation which, lacking natural resources, must live by its wits. (Rohlen 1988: 25)

Under the present system, compulsory education (nine years) terminates upon completion of junior high school (age 15). 'Japanese children attend school about 50 more days each year, which means that by high school graduation they have been in school the equivalent of three to four more years than their American counterparts' (ibid.). There is little reluctance in attending school, to the point where drop-outs and illiteracy are practically nonexistent. Since textbooks and curriculum are nationally approved the level of education is uniform, which allows all children in each grade to study essentially the same lessons at the same pace throughout the country.

> The students within one class are divided into small groups of mixed ability. In this way the quick learners are able to help the slower learners. When called on by the teacher to answer a question, a student usually will turn to his or her neighbors to check the answer before responding. This style of answering by group consensus is considered not only acceptable but the norm .... In Japan students generally are promoted en masse. It is considered the responsibility of the fast learners to teach the slow learners. Responding to the needs of both types of students are the increasingly prevalent special private schools called *juku*, attended after the regular school day and on weekends. Here the remedial learner can get extra tutoring, while the advanced learner can move ahead .... The qualities hoped for in a Japanese child ... are cooperativeness, diligence and perseverance. (Green 1989: 3 and 6)

Secondary education ends with the completion of senior high school (three years). Such schools are ranked academically or according to specialization – for example, commercial or technical high schools. Entrance examinations are required for admission. Education beyond the high-school level takes the form of vocational schools, junior colleges and universities. Attending a university, of which there are close to 500, is a full-time proposition generally ending with the degree of Bachelor of Arts (BA) or Sciences (BS), the average age of graduates being 22–3 years.

> In March 1989, 2.9% of junior high school graduates took a full-time job. Of the senior high school graduates 35.6% entered the labor market and over one-half went on to continue their education (JIL 1990b: 3).
> In 1987, among the latter,
> > 18% entered a 4-year university, of whom 1/3 were female;
> > 12% entered a 2-year junior college, of whom 94% were female, and
> > 27% went to vocational schools, of whom 39% were female.
> > (MOE 1988: 590–600)

Few university students go on to graduate school, mostly because of the industry's eagerness in signing them up as new employees even before they graduate, a selection process which does not favour master's or doctorate degree holders. (But it should be noted that about one-third of the 13,000 or so Japanese students in American universities are pursuing higher degrees.)

> Science and engineering are the only branches of study in which graduate schools have developed for reasons other than apprentice training for the academic profession or to provide a haven for those who want to postpone choice of a career. Engineering masters *do* confer a career advantage, and do so increasingly as knowledge becomes more specialized and the R & D establishments of Japanese firms which look for masters and PhDs expand.... The advantage of getting recruits earlier at the BA stage, and starting them earlier on all the specific learning they had to do, was seen to outweigh the deepening and broadening of theoretical understanding which a Master's course would offer. Some firms still hold the same view, but preference, and career advantage, is now increasingly given to holders of Master's degrees – almost universally for those entering the R & D departments of large firms, less universally for those entering production departments. (Dore and Sako 1989: 52 and 78)

By and large, compared to other industrial countries, Japan benefits from one of the best educated industrial labour forces. This is the reason why

> the development of wide-ranged skills may be most effectively used for continual environmental changes. In the longer run, however, when technological progress necessitates changes in the design of machinery and process, versatility and a deeper understanding of the technological process on the part of workers may help them adapt to a new process as well as start a new process without being interrupted by a reorganizational interim period. (Aoki 1988: 39)

Social dynamics

The other foundation on which Japan built the development of its human resources is the nature of its social dynamics. Japanese social behaviour is usually described as group-oriented but this needs to be understood from a Japanese point of view. First, let us take the Western 'group' which is based upon individuals according to the pattern

$$(1) + (1) + (1) + (1) + (1) + \ldots \ = \ GROUP$$

The Japanese, however, view the 'group' as a community which has a different pattern:

$$COMMUNITY = 1 \times 1 \times 1 \times 1 \times 1 \times \ldots$$

Whereas the premise of the Western group, the individual *qua* individual, tends almost to deny the group, the dynamism of the Japanese *community* is reinforced by the individual *qua* member of the community. The key factor here is interdependence. Pressure on the individual to conform to communal norms is expected; yet the younger generation is seen as rebellious and anxious to display non-conformism. Some authors find this a valid reason for criticizing as shallow the *democracy* of postwar Japan. They contend that there are some coercive forces at work among the many aspects of education, corporate life, and social behaviour (McCormack and Sugimoto 1986).

One common explanation of Japanese social dynamics places significance on the fact that the cultivation of rice, given climatic and other conditions peculiar to Japan, was by necessity a communal affair.

> There is no doubt that through centuries of agrarian experience up to as recently as a generation ago, the Japanese developed the customs of mutual help, collective coordination, risk sharing, ad hoc and flexible adaptation to continual and incremental environmental changes, diligent work habits, and penetration of communal life into the private sphere, which are now viewed as characteristics of modern Japanese factory life. (Aoki 1988: 307)

In addition, such a close, if not closed, type of social dynamics has been greatly reinforced by at least three significant factors:

1 Throughout its long historical record, Japan has never been invaded, except in 1945;
2 From 1632 to 1854, Japanese were prohibited to leave the country and no foreigners were permitted to enter, with the exception of a few Dutch and Chinese traders; and
3 At the end of 1988, of the total population of about 125 million, only 941,005 (0.8 per cent) were registered as non-Japanese residents. This figure represents 677,140 Koreans, 129,269 Chinese, 32,766 Americans, 32,185 Filipinos, and 22,027 Europeans (JETRO 1990: 132).

To be Japanese is much more than a reflection of statehood (*nation* is too recent an historical development to be used here, as most historians see this notion starting in the seventeenth century). The Japanese had been Japanese for many centuries before they acquired their so-called present-day, Western-inspired nationality. The Japanese self-identity, in order to survive through the centuries, required flexibility in adjusting to constantly changing circumstances. In Japan, the tradition was and continues to be, to change. It was then not *Japan* as a political entity that allowed the Japanese to survive but that they learned to rely on themselves. For instance, in the crucial decades that launched industrialization (1868–95), Japan did not rely on foreign capital but achieved it on the basis of domestic capital accumulation.

MODERNIZATION

A commercial economy thrived during the Tokugawa era (1600–1868), but industry was almost nonexistent. The Meiji Restoration (1868) launched industrialization in the form of a national emergency in order to resist the threat of Western powers and continued in this manner to overcome the country's lack of primary resources and maintain standards of living. But contrary to the Western example of modernization, industry was not promoted by the private sector but by the government. What was soon to become *private* industry, first began as a *public* mission. 'Japanese spirit, Western techniques' (*wakon yôsai*), the Meiji slogan of modernization, held implications for the Japanese that to remain Japanese they had to import Western institutions and techniques. More than ten centuries ago, when the Japanese decided to become *modern* it meant to adopt Chinese civilization. This was done on a grandiose scale, but not at the cost of becoming Chinese. In the last century, the process was repeated with regard to Western industrialism, but not at the cost of becoming Western. A surprising social capacity to absorb Western technology was revealed

1 In its selection of appropriate technology, starting with textiles, then heavy industry, and now knowledge-intensive industries;
2 In its adjustment to domestic factor proportions and development of human resources; and
3 In its improvement of technical applications, for example, miniaturization.

In recent years, however, not much technology remains to be *borrowed* from the West; Japan is now on its own. Since 1972, albeit on an annual rather than aggregate basis, Japan has enjoyed a positive balance in technology trade (Wheeler *et al.* 1982: 126). In addition, a significant shift towards basic research has recently been noted.

Today, a less cohesive younger generation is rapidly replacing the relatively small group of personalities who rebuilt postwar Japan. However, the changes are not all new – they do reflect many of the same 'standard' elements. In line with the human-resource orientation of their industrialization, the Japanese have had to create appropriate institutional innovations stressing interdependence in order to succeed in modernization and to achieve their current economic status. The entire economy revolves around three forms of interdependence:

1 Interdependence between government and business;
2 Interdependence between companies; and
3 Interdependence between management and workforce.

All three are highly dynamic and undergo constant change in reaction to circumstances both domestic and international. They are described in more detail below.

Interdependence between government and business

A relationship reminiscent of early industrialization characterized and implemented by governmental institutions was repeated after World War II when US-sponsored reforms were to be carried out by the existing bureaucracy. Later, the image of 'Japan Inc.' was much used and, in some cases, abused. Johnson proposed a distinction between a regulatory state, a form more commonly found in Western societies, and a developmental state, which has been a characteristic of the Japanese economy for most of its modern history.

> The issue is not one of state intervention in the economy. All states intervene in their economies for various reasons.... The question is how the government intervenes and for what purposes.... A regulatory, or market-rational, state concerns itself with the forms and procedures – the rules, if you will – of economic competition, but it does not concern itself with substantive matters.... The developmental, or plan-rational, state, by contrast, has as its dominant feature precisely the setting of such substantive social and economic goals. Another way to make this distinction is to consider a state's priorities in economic policy. In the plan-rational state, the government will give greatest precedence to industrial policy, that is, to a concern with the structure of domestic industry and with promoting the structure that enhances the nation's international competitiveness.... On the other hand, the market-rational state usually will not even have an industrial policy (or, at any rate, will not recognize it as such). Instead, both its domestic and foreign economic policy, including its trade policy, will stress rules and reciprocal concessions (although perhaps influenced by some goals that are not industrially specific, goals such as price stability or full employment). Its trade policy will normally be subordinate to general foreign policy, being used more often to cement political relationships than to obtain strictly economic advantages. (Johnson 1982: 17–20)

Current manifestations of the interdependence of government and business are numerous. Deliberation boards (*shingikai*) created at the initiative of the bureaucracy and composed of experts as well as representatives of the sectors affected, review and provide advice on all significant policy considerations (Sone 1989: 277–82). Administrative guidance (*gyôsei shidô*) is in the form of constant interaction between bureaucrats and industry. Trade associations, of which many originated in the prewar years of cartel predominance, and business

organizations are vital communications channels linking the author-
ities and industry, to the extent that an already obscure distinction
between public and private activities is even further blurred (Samuels
1987; Lynn and McKeown 1988). The bureaucracy tends to look at
business as a partner to encourage rather than as an outsider who
needs to be controlled. The modern legal system itself, imported into
Japan about a century ago, did not supplant indigenous values
(Chapter 8).

Interdependence between companies

Notwithstanding the fierce competition that prevails on the Japanese
market, close cooperation among corporations is also clearly evident.
In prewar years, interdependence within the *zaibatsu* was controlled
by a family-held holding company, but today, in the *keiretsu* (industrial groupings), interdependence is the result not of control but of
cooperation. The general trading company (*sôgô shôsha*) brings into
the industrial group a substantial number of smaller firms which
receive its help both business-wise and financially. The general
acceptance of interdependence between parent companies and their
subsidiaries, subcontracting between manufacturers and suppliers
(Chapter 8), and interdependence of manufacturers, wholesalers and
retailers, if not also customers (Chapter 9), dictates most of the flow
of business. Business organizations and trade associations actively
integrate the often divergent interests of individual companies.

Interdependence between management and workforce

Management and labour are partners in business. Cultural values
stemming from an agrarian heritage as mentioned earlier have often
been used to explain the sense of obligation coupled with membership in a company, the importance attached to intragroup behaviour,
and the reliance placed on the company for one's quality of life.
Some experts, though, object to such views on the grounds that it can
all be explained on the basis of economic rationality. The fact is that
most Japanese do expect long-term security from their workplace and
readily display corporate pride, whereas Western counterparts would
take pride in the occupation they hold. Hence the postwar innovation
in the form of labour organization known as enterprise unionism
arises (Chapter 3). The outcome – a very effective style of corporate
organization (Chapter 5).

INDUSTRIAL STRUCTURE

Japan numbers well over 6 million business establishments, almost half of them in wholesale and retail trade. As shown in Table 1.1, in 1980, 1.5 million and in 1988, 1.8 million of them were registered companies, out of which about 1 million were capitalized at ¥5 million or less. Thus what seems to be a permanent characteristic of Japan's industrial structure is the small/medium enterprise (SME) sector, and its importance in the economy is overwhelming. Government policies are in fact providing vital support to this sector (Calder 1988).

The Small and Medium Enterprise Basic Law (1963, revised in 1973) provides the following definitions of incorporated small and medium enterprises (which, however, are not consistently followed by government agencies): in manufacturing, fewer than 300 regular workers, or capitalized at less than ¥100 million; in wholesale, fewer than 100 regular workers, or capitalized at less than ¥30 million; in retailing, fewer than 50 regular workers, or capitalized at less than ¥10 million. (In general, the firm's size is given by the number of its regular employees.)

Not widely appreciated in terms of Japan's human resource development is the fact that SMEs stand for an overwhelming majority of enterprises and employees. If the definition of 'capitalized at less than ¥100 million' is used, in 1980, out of less than 1 million companies 17,000 were large and in 1988, out of 1.8 million 23,000 were large. If the definition of 'less than 300 regular workers' is used, out of 6.5 million private business establishments only 8,000 are large, employing 5.6 million out of a total of 49 million (Table 1.2). In manufacturing, for example, in the early 1980s nearly 60 per cent

Table 1.1 Number of companies by capitalization, 1980–8

Capitalization (million yen)	1980	1986	1987	1988
5 or less	961,580	1,031,621	1,049,935	1,064,585
Over 5–10	237,674	321,698	358,655	383,142
Over 10–100	233,947	327,539	352,527	380,213
Over 100–1,000	14,066	17,740	19,097	20,242
Over 1,000	2,282	3,044	3,220	3,491
Total	1,449,549	1,701,642	1,783,434	1,851,673
1978 = 100	107	126	132	137

Source: National Tax Administration 1990: 10

Table 1.2 Number of private establishments and persons engaged, 1966–86 (in thousands)

Size of establishment	Private establishments			Persons engaged		
	1966	*1975*	*1986*	*1966*	*1975*	*1986*
Total	4,239	5,408	6,512	31,256	39,853	49,225
1–4	3,086	3,849	4,434	6,276	8,005	9,502
5–9	609	838	1,123	3,914	5,380	7,245
10–29	390	526	710	6,230	8,337	11,216
30–49	75	97	124	2,808	3,618	4,682
50–99	48	61	76	3,281	4,103	5,135
100–299	24	30	37	3,851	4,689	5,762
300–499	3.5	4.0	4.5	1,309	1,501	1,709
500–999	2.0	2.4	2.4	1,331	1,623	1,652
1,000 or more	1.1	1.2	1.1	2,257	2,597	2,323

Source: Statistics Bureau 1990: 120–1

of the labour force found employment in enterprises with less than 100 workers in contrast to the US and the UK, where this figure barely exceeded 25 per cent (MITI 1986: 15).

Now that Japan has caught up with existing models of modernization, it continues the process on its own and, more than ever, is stressing the development of its only reliable resource – people. It is aiming at what it calls *jôhô shakai* (information society). Here, the foundation is explicitly built upon human resources, namely the knowledge-intensive industries. Currently, the restructuring of the economy implies diversification and the development of new products and services on a large scale.

In the manufacturing sector, the materials industries are planning to move into fields related to new industrial areas and biotechnology. In the processing industries, companies are planning to move into areas such as microelectronics, information and communications, etc. . . . . In the non-manufacturing sector, business enterprises are showing interest in leisure, information and communications, housing, and the senior citizen markets, as well as urban development . . . . Corporate strategies have become even more aggressive under the pressure of the strong yen, and these efforts have contributed to sustain the economic growth led by domestic demand. Certainly, substitution of non-profitable areas by imports, and substitution of exports by overseas local production,

Table 1.3 Economic trends among major developed countries, 1978–89 (per cent)

Country	Average 1978–82	Average 1983–7	1987	1988 (est.)	1989 (est.)
Japan					
Growth rate	4.5	4.0	4.2	4.1	3.8
Unemployment rate	2.2	2.7	2.8	2.8	3.0
Inflation rate	2.9	1.0	−0.1	1.2	1.5
USA					
Growth rate	1.6	3.8	2.9	2.9	2.7
Unemployment rate*	7.3	7.5	6.2	6.0	5.9
Inflation rate	8.2	3.3	3.0	3.2	3.5
W. Germany					
Growth rate	1.6	2.3	1.7	1.7	1.7
Unemployment rate	4.4	8.0	7.9	8.1	8.2
Inflation rate	4.3	2.5	2.1	2.0	2.0
Average for developed economies					
Growth rate	2.1	3.3	3.1	2.8	2.6
Unemployment rate	6.2	8.9	7.6	7.4	7.4
Inflation rate	8.1	3.9	2.9	3.0	3.1

Note: *The concept in use differs from country to country, so a margin of variance should be made for international comparison.
Source: EPA 1988: 180

are negative factors from the view of domestic production. Their impact must be assessed carefully. It is, however, reasonable to conclude that corporate activities have been bringing about structural changes, while avoiding "the hollowing out phenomenon". (EPA 1988: 120–3)

The strength of the Japanese economy is indeed impressive. It clearly outperformed the other developed economies (Table 1.3) and may continue to do so for the foreseeable future. This is the challenge that Japanese and non-Japanese corporations alike must face.

FOREIGN FIRMS IN JAPAN

Foreign firms have been active in Japan since the opening of the country to foreign trade (1854), particularly Western trading companies. In the early decades of this century foreign manufacturing interests were established which included Babcock & Wilcox, Dunlop, General Electric and Western Electric. After World War I, the newcomers were Canada Aluminum, Ford, General Motors, Siemens, Westinghouse, etc. As of January 1931, 88 foreign direct investments (manufacturing) were reported. There were also a few foreign establishments in oil and food industries and international trade (Yuzawa and Udagawa 1990).

An exact count of foreign firms in Japan today is not available. One problem lies in defining them properly, as can be seen by the following results:

- The *Ministry of Finance* (MOF) covers cases of foreign direct investment in Japan. In the fiscal year ending 31 March 1989, it reported that total foreign direct investment jumped 46.5 per cent in value and 8.2 per cent in the number of investments over the previous fiscal year. Cumulatively there were 31,508 cases, amounting to a total value of US$12.8 billion (MITI 1989c: 11).

- The *Ministry of International Trade and Industry* (MITI) conducts an annual survey of so-called foreign capital affiliated firms. Its definition in terms of foreign capital ratio has varied over time: 15 per cent in 1967, 20 per cent from 1968 to 1974, 25 per cent from 1975 to 1981, and 50 per cent since 1982. In 1985 it sent out questionnaires to 2,556 companies, of which 1,132 responded (MITI 1987a: 7); in 1988 questionnaires were sent to 2,674 companies and 1,401 responded (MITI 1990c: 1). But the MITI surveys exclude the following industries that are not under its jurisdiction: finance, insurance, transportation, telecommunications, real estate, construction, and agriculture, forestry and fishery.

- For its part, the *Ministry of Labour* (MOL) periodically conducts a survey of labour–management relations in foreign affiliated firms. In 1983 such firms were defined as having more than a 25 per cent foreign capital ratio and in 1987 more than 50 per cent, but the survey also included branches and offices of foreign corporations. In 1987 it mailed 2,650 survey forms and received 1,178 responses (MOL 1988b: 1).

A decade ago, in fiscal 1979, based on *Fortune*'s annual listing of the top 200 non-financial US companies, 127 (63.5 per cent) had operations in Japan, each running an average of 3.9 subsidiaries and joint ventures. Of the top 100 non-American corporations, excluding the 19 companies which were Japanese, 28 (34.6 per cent) were active in Japan with an average of 7.2 subsidiaries (JETRO 1982: 6). Currently, only a hundred or so of the largest US companies, as ranked by sales in *Fortune*'s 500 listing, are represented in Japan (ACCJ 1988).

> The explanation for this paradox of strikingly low foreign direct investment in a notably attractive economy lies in the issue of acquisition. The build-up of the substantial position of U.S. companies in Western Europe in the 1950s and 1960s was largely accomplished through acquisition of attractive and successful European companies by U.S. companies, which could then build on the acquired base with capital and technology. Likewise, over the past decade or so, European firms aiming to build a position in the United States have generally done so through acquiring successful or promising U.S. firms. (Abegglen 1984: 126)

On a cumulative basis, US direct investment represents 49.0 per cent of total foreign direct investments; the total for Europe is 23.6 per cent, Switzerland being the largest European investor (7.3 per cent) (MITI 1989c: 12). Recent foreign direct investment has been in the form of: '(1) high level of manufacturing investment in high-tech areas including electronics, computers, and pharmaceuticals; (2) active investment in research and development accompanying invest-ment in high-tech areas; (3) Western companies which formerly had only a presence in Japan through agents have now switched to the establishment of sales subsidiaries in Japan in order to respond to the expansion of domestic demand with a posture of direct marketing' (JETRO 1989b: 115). The fastest increase in direct foreign invest-ment is seen in manufacturing. As of June 1988, the cumulative number of manufacturing plants (with 50 per cent or more foreign ownership) totalled 216 (JETRO 1989a: 11).

Table 1.4 Profitability, pay-out ratio and dividend rate in all firms and in foreign firms, FY 1985–8 (per cent)

Fiscal year (April–March)	Profitability		Pay-out ratio		Dividend rate	
	All firms	Foreign firms	All firms	Foreign firms	All firms	Foreign firms
1985	2.0	4.2	32.7	69.5	8.3	23.7
1986	2.0	5.3	34.6	69.5	8.0	34.8
1987	2.5	6.1	26.6	68.6	8.1	22.7
1988	2.8	6.8	25.9	67.3	8.0	25.7

Source: MITI 1990a: 10

According to MITI, of the foreign firms surveyed, total sales in FY 1988 was 1.0 per cent of the total sales of all corporations in the same industries, but by separate industries the figure was 2.3 per cent in the manufacturing sector (petroleum has always been an exception, with 26.9 per cent, assets amounting to one-quarter of total assets in the industry) and 0.6 per cent in the commerce sector (MITI 1990c: 4). For many years, however, their profitability has been higher than that of domestic firms (Table 1.4).

> For the period 1966–1977, U.S. direct manufacturing investment abroad achieved an aggregate average apparent return on investment (ROI) of 12.4 per cent with Japan having the highest ROI of 19.0 per cent. Similarly, in the apparent ROI of U.K. companies, aggregate averages for the years 1974 and 1977 were 13.2 per cent and 13.1 per cent respectively, while their ROI in Japan for the same years was 29.7 per cent and 34.5 per cent respectively (ACCJ 1979: 65 and 67). The U.S. Department of Commerce reported that the ROI for U.S. direct investment abroad in 1985 totaled 14.8 per cent and that Japan's ROI was the highest at 17.5 per cent (Booz, Allen & Hamilton 1987: A–28). Not surprisingly, in 1987 over 40 per cent, and in 1988 one-third of the foreign firms responding to the surveys conducted by MITI selected the growth potential of Japan's markets as their prime motive for doing business in Japan (MITI 1989a: 188 and 1990c: 162).

None the less, more than 90 per cent of foreign firms had less than 300 employees (in fact, at least 80 per cent of them had less than 100 employees), thus placing them under the Japanese definition of small/medium enterprise. In March 1988 of 1,257 foreign firms participating in the MITI survey, 524 employed less than ten people and 95 employed 300 or more (MITI 1990c: 26–7).

In facing local competitors, large or small, the smaller size of the average foreign firm in Japan is definitely a handicap, and neither the size of the home office nor the corporation's international standing can compensate for this disadvantage. The expatriate executive and, even more so, his home office may try to argue against this point, but most likely in vain.

In the latest study sponsored by the American Chamber of Commerce in Japan and the Council of the European Business Community, the following conclusion was presented:

> Overall, the major barriers to investment in Japan relate mostly to operating problems in starting up and sustaining a profitable

business, rather than any legal or regulatory restrictions imposed by the Japanese government. Japan is a difficult place for a foreign company to do business, and many companies perceive that these difficulties cannot be overcome by simply investing more money to solve the problem.... Many foreign companies are restructuring their presence in Japan as part of their efforts to redirect their strategy and approach to the Japan market. (Booz, Allen & Hamilton 1987: 25 and 47)

2 Employment and hiring

Japanese statistics on employment cover three categories: self-employed, family members, and employees (Table 2.1). Of the 9 million plus self-employed a large percentage are owner-operators of either small family enterprises or unincorporated businesses. For most of them their major asset is a small plot of land that may perhaps be seen as compensating for their lack of true entrepreneurship as well as other shortcomings they may have. Furthermore, they can always fall back on a lenient enforcement of tax reporting requirements. In 1987, 12.7 per cent of the working population were self-employed in Japan, compared to 10.6 per cent in France and the United Kingdom, 8.1 per cent in West Germany, and 7.5 per cent in the United States (OECD 1989: 14–15).

The majority of those categorized as 'family members', most of whom are women, are employed in either agriculture or wholesale/retail trade. In incorporated as well as unincorporated enterprises, their wages, if paid at all, are tax deductible under certain conditions. In 1988, about 5.5 million family workers were recorded.

In the third category of employment, 'employees' in 1988 rose to more than 45 million, of whom over 35 per cent were female, which is not unlike the trend in other industrial countries (*ibid.*: 11). This category is split into two basic types of wage-earners: regular (permanent) and non-regular (temporary or daily). Over 40 million are regular employees hired with the understanding that, in principle, employment starts immediately after graduation and continues until the mandatory age limit (*teinen*) which is mostly 60, and that compensation and promotion are based on a combination of performance and length of service (Chapter 4). Such is the *norm*, however not necessarily the practice, say, in the smaller business establishments.

The line between temporary and part-time employees is not distinguished clearly, but part-time generally refers to those who worked

Table 2.1 Employed persons, 1985–9 (in thousands)

Employment	1985		1988		1989	
	All	Female	All	Female	All	Female
All industries	58,070	23,040	60,110	24,080	61,280	24,740
Self-employed	9,160	2,880	9,100	2,840	8,960	2,810
Family workers	5,590	4,610	5,430	4,480	5,310	4,370
Employees	43,130	1,548	45,380	16,700	46,790	17,490
Regular	38,660	12,470	40,540	13,430	41,760	14,070
Temporary	3,210	2,370	3,600	2,620	3,760	2,760
Daily	1,260	650	1,240	650	1,270	660

Source: Statistics Bureau 1990: 72–3

less than 35 hours during the survey week. Three-quarters of the temporary and part-time employees work in small firms (see Chalmers 1989: 76–108). In larger firms they are hired basically at the discretion of the company under a labour contract (which is renewable) for a period less than one year. A common practice is to hire such employees more or less on a regular basis, which shows a certain degree of stability in employment (since under normal conditions the contract will be renewed), but working conditions in these cases are inferior to those of regular employees. 'The ratio of part-timers for 1989 was 3.93, up 0.85 percent points over the previous year. It was the highest rate recorded since 1972 when the Ministry [of Labour] began conducting the survey' (JIL 1990: 3).

Until the mid-1970s temporary employment was, at least for male employees, a stepping stone to regular employment. These two types of employment, regular and temporary, are now distinctly set apart, as is obvious in the case of working women. Their pattern of employment is substantially different from that of men. Upon graduation, women may be hired as regular employees, but in general they are expected to quit at the time of marriage or childbirth, usually about the age of 25; later, around the age of 40, when they return to the labour market, they are hired as non-regular employees. Currently, one-third of the female labour force is employed part-time; of the part-timers, one woman out of three in fact works full-time, continuously renewing her contract over a period of several years without the benefits given to regular employees. An Equal Opportunity Law was enacted in 1985; its effective administration is only beginning.

Traditionally, when the labour demand slackened, a large proportion of female workers who failed to find a job were discouraged
from continuing their search and retired from the labour market.
But recent studies suggest that the effect of 'discouragement' is
becoming weaker and the phenomenon of 'involuntary' part-time
workers has become more common. There is a growing tendency
among female workers to prefer working to leisure, and to stay in
the labour market in order to seek an alternative job even if the
prospects are not bright. Some may remain unemployed, but many
are likely to be absorbed in part-time jobs as (subjectively) trans-
itory measures. (Aoki 1988: 172–3)

UNEMPLOYMENT AND LABOUR MOBILITY

'If official statistics on employment and unemployment are any guide
to the degree of labour market efficiency, the performance of the
Japanese labour market is almost miraculous' (Taira 1983: 3). The
average unemployment rate for the advanced economies was 8.9 per
cent between 1983 and 1987, but only 2.7 per cent in Japan (see
Table 1.3). In 1989, the rate was 2.3 per cent, which represented
about 1.5 million unemployed, the lowest annual average since 1981,
when it stood at 2.2 per cent (JIL 1990: 3).

A statistic often disputed in Japan as it is elsewhere, unemployment rate, reflects different categories of people in different ways.
Female unemployment, for instance, is twice that of their male
counterparts and is higher among the young and aged workers than
the middle-aged.

One reason that restraining employment at large firms does not
cause massive unemployment is that there are alternative ways to
absorb employment. First, leaving aside the effect of labour-saving
technology and organizational innovation ... the large firms have
been able to reduce employment by simplifying the hierarchical
layers, hiving off subsidiaries ... and relying on subcontracting
(outsourcing)....

Second, the low level of unemployment may be partly attribut-
able to the absorption of the potentially unemployed into other
categories of disadvantaged workers. In the great surges of growth
after 1955 large firms hired many of their new workers on
temporary contracts of three months to one year, which could be
renewed at management's discretion.... [Later] many temporary
workers at large firms were either promoted to the status of regular

workers or quit voluntarily to seek relatively better-paid jobs at other firms (not rarely at small firms). By the early 1970s, the use of temporary workers as a ploy to maintain a buffer group of long-term but lower-paid workers had largely disappeared.

Recently, however, a new category of workers who are employed for relatively shorter periods has arisen: these are part-time workers, predominantly middle-aged females particularly in relatively smaller firms in the service, wholesale, and retail industries.... (Aoki 1988: 171–2)

Unemployment, especially in Japan, is also affected by labour mobility. In 1984, about 32 per cent of all male workers aged 50 to 54 were still working for the same company that they joined upon graduation. International comparison shows that the percentage of employees who remained at their current job for 20 years or more was 21.9 per cent in Japan, 13.2 per cent in France, 12.1 per cent in the United Kingdom, 11.6 per cent in West Germany, and 9.9 per cent in the United States (OECD 1986: 68). On the other hand, in Japan there are roughly as many who leave their jobs as are hired annually. Of those who leave, two-thirds are in the small/medium-enterprise sector, often in the wholesale and retail trade; in addition, about one-half are women and 20 per cent are part-time employees. Thus the smaller the firm the greater the turnover, particularly among younger employees (Table 2.2). '[Y]oung workers in small plants move from one firm to another so frequently that the annual separation rates are more than 30 per cent. Although these rates drop to about 15 per cent when these workers are in their thirties and forties,

Table 2.2 Manufacturing: ratio of retained employees (male) by size of enterprise, 1977–87 (per cent)

Age bracket	1,000 or more regular employees		100–999 regular employees		10–99 regular employees	
	1977–82	*1982–7*	*1977–82*	*1982–7*	*1977–82*	*1982–7*
25–9	79.1	91.3	68.2	70.6	58.0	50.5
30–4	83.6	90.1	81.1	86.9	74.2	69.2
35–9	90.0	91.2	88.4	93.7	82.0	78.6
40–4	92.5	88.6	92.6	95.3	86.9	81.9
45–9	90.5	88.1	91.2	89.4	86.1	84.1
50–4	89.9	77.6	83.9	82.7	80.6	77.4

Source: MOL 1988c: 189

Table 2.3 Employment adjustment measures in large companies, 1974–5 and 1985–6 (per cent of companies)

Employment adjustment measures	Companies listed on the Tokyo Stock Exchange (1974–5)	Large manufacturing companies	
		1985	*1986*
Transfer of personnel	–	43.4	49.3
Cut of overtime work	75.3	26.6	33.9
Dismissal of part-time employees	59.6	22.6	27.6
Reduction of management compensation	56.1	22.4	21.2
Stop of managerial promotion	24.3	11.6	12.2
Call for early separation	14.2	11.6	10.5
Promotion of voluntary separation	–	6.2	7.6
Temporary layoff	40.6	5.4	5.4
Dismissal	5.2	2.6	2.2
No pay increase for general employees	1.5	1.5	1.5

Source: MITI 1976 and MITI 1987b: 83

they are still about 10 percentage points higher than the rate of Japanese workers in large enterprises' (Koike 1983: 97).

However, the employment system is put under constant pressure by business fluctuations as the accepted norm of regular employment tends to make labour costs fixed rather than variable. In contrast to part-time employees, regular employees cannot be dismissed except under extreme circumstances and when they are a substantial premium is added to their separation allowance, which is a major consideration of their salary system (Chapter 4). Adjusting employment to business fluctuations is done in various ways including, as a last recourse, dismissal. In recent years, the economy went through two critical periods, the oil crisis of 1973 and the rapid appreciation of the yen in 1985. In large companies adjustment measures were taken, as described in Table 2.3. Special attention should be paid to the temporary reduction of management compensation (Chapter 6).

AGEING WORKFORCE

The Japanese system of employment, which depends on regular employment as its mainstay, forces companies to be invariably concerned with the average age of their employees. Traditionally, listed corporations include this average age in their financial statements as a key to assessing general conditions of the company. Recent developments have made a rapidly ageing work force a basic issue in corporate policy:

1 Under the high economic growth of the 1960s graduates were hired in greater numbers; this trend was drastically reversed with the slower growth rate in the 1970s;
2 Largely under pressure from the labour unions, more and more companies extended the mandatory age limit from 55 to 60 years;
3 A rapid increase in the general age of the population raised life-expectancy to one of the highest in the world, as the averages given below indicate:

Year	Male	Female
1960	65.32	70.19
1970	69.31	74.66
1989	75.91	81.77

Source: Keizai Koho Center 1991: 9

Average life-expectancy is estimated to increase steadily: in the year 2010 the figures are expected to rise to 78.76 for men and 85.95 years for women (JIL 1989b: 2). Since 1965 the average age of the labour force increased from 31.7 to 38.2 and years of service from 6.6 to 10.8 (MOL 1990b: 2). In the large manufacturing companies, average years of service between 1976 and 1986 increased from 12.0 to 17.4, an increase of 5.4 years (MITI 1987b: 67).

Older age means longer length of service and thus a higher salary, particularly at larger firms. It may also mean the loss of what has long been considered a major motivating factor, namely the prospect for managerial promotion (Amaya 1983: 25) (Chapter 6). In terms of the labour market, control of the average age of the workforce has been, in the past as well as the present, a reason why Japanese competitors concentrate on hiring new graduates.

HIRING NEW SCHOOL GRADUATES

About 4 million employees are newly hired each year (Table 2.4). An important distinction is made between inexperienced and experienced candidates. Half of the inexperienced market is comprised of new graduates and the other half of those who, for some reason or another, delayed their entrance into the labour market or re-entered

Table 2.4 Newly hired employees, 1986–8 (in thousands)

Newly hired employees	1986		1987		1988	
	Number	(Female)	Number	(Female)	Number	(Female)
Total	3,914	(2,057)	3,998	(2,121)	4,549	(2,380)
Occupationally:						
Inexperienced	1,872	(1,158)	1,884	(1,162)	2,066	(1,287)
New graduates	984	(503)	967	(526)	988	(520)
Others	887	(655)	917	(636)	1,078	(766)
Experienced	2,042	(898)	2,114	(959)	2,482	(1,093)
New graduates Size of establishment						
1,000 and more	296	(150)	249	(133)	247	(121)
300–999	207	(107)	183	(101)	201	(112)
100–299	196	(97)	203	(101)	211	(107)
30–99	131	(67)	143	(63)	181	(95)
5–29	127	(6)	153	(103)	124	(72)

Sources: MOL 1989h: 26–8 and previous years

the labour market after some interruption (e.g. women who left their jobs to take care of their children). The experienced market, on the other hand, is comprised of employees hired in mid-career (*chûto saiyô*).

One of the characteristics of regular employment is that hiring takes place at the time the candidate graduates from school – i.e., when he is ready to enter the labour market. In Japan, the academic year begins in April and ends in March. The hiring of these graduates thus takes place on 1 April. In 1988, about 1 million of those newly graduated were hired (of whom half were female), out of which only 45,000 took employment immediately after junior high school, while over 525,000 were senior high school graduates and 420,000 were junior college or university graduates (MOL 1989h: 27).

Recruitment of high school graduates is mostly done through two main routes. One is through the Public Employment Security Office (PESO), to which companies submit a recruitment card for each job opening with a description of the position, company, terms and conditions which must then be approved by PESO. These cards are also used by schools for their own referral assistance. The other route is through the school's Placement Office, which companies can contact directly. Schools also provide additional assistance to prospective graduates such as giving a sample company entrance examination and interview. Applications are accepted in September. By mid-November most students have received confirmation of their employment to commence in April.

PESO is never used as a method of recruiting from colleges, either for two-year junior colleges or four-year universities; these graduates are recruited by corporate headquarters. Prospective graduates apply through their school's Placement Office, through some personal connection (often a professor, particularly for science graduates), or directly to the company (this has recently become more common, but not at prestigious institutions and companies) by contacting certain alumni or acquaintances in the company. Companies pay less attention to the academic discipline in which the candidate graduated, except in the area of physical sciences, and place more emphasis on university reputation, which they use as an indicator of the long-term potential of the newly hired employee.

Though not too successful, attempts to regulate the scramble for prospective university graduates have been pursued. Major firms had actually agreed that direct contact with students would not be initiated until 1 October and that recruitment examinations would begin on 1 November. But the fact remains that by the end of September or even earlier, all good candidates have somehow been confirmed; examinations and interviews which follow are, in essence, just a formality. In order to sustain the interest of selected candidates, companies plan various activities (meetings, seminars, publication of newsletters, etc.) during the six months or so that preceed formal hiring. On 1 April they are welcomed by the company president and several directors at a formal gathering. Thus starts an intensive period of several weeks to several months (but only a few days for female recruits) of indoctrination and socialization. The new recruits are assembled for several days at some company resort where they undergo what has been nicknamed 'skinship' (since they eat together, sleep together, exercise together, etc.) and where lectures are given by various managers and by others from outside the company. A strong bond prevails for years afterwards among those who join the company in the same year.

In Matsushita, the orientation and training of new employees from universities (about 800 persons) are centralized in the head office and the training is conducted as follows: lectures in the head office, three weeks; training in retail stores, three months; training in the works, one month; lectures on cost accounting, one month;

lectures on marketing, two months. After this eight-month training new graduates are distributed to various departments and subsidiaries. (Kono 1984: 320)

Back at the office or factory, senior employees expect to rely on the system which they had already been through in their school days, the *sempai–kôhai* (senior–junior) relationship. But the overall intensity of such corporate socialization is questioned these days by a growing number of the younger entrants into the company ... until they themselves gain the status of having seniority.

Remarkably in line with the practices of regular employment, university graduates are not granted special treatment; they start training at the bottom. This means that in automobile manufacturing they spend several months on the production line; in a bank they are sent out to collect deposits; and in a private railway company they punch passenger tickets.

MID-CAREER HIRING

Mid-career hiring occurs more frequently among smaller firms where mobility is greater (Table 2.5). Technology and competition are, however, forcing larger companies to bring in outside expertise, which is done on a limited basis. Human resources required for corporate diversification are primarily sought internally from among regular employees or at least from within the enterprise group, as an

Table 2.5 Manufacturing: ratio of mid-career hired employees (male) by size of enterprise and age bracket, 1977–87 (per cent)

Age bracket	1,000 or more*		100–999		10–99	
	1977–82	1982–7	1977–82	1982–7	1977–82	1982–7
25–9	1.1	1.7	4.9	4.0	12.1	11.2
30–4	0.4	0.6	3.0	2.3	8.6	7.9
35–9	0.3	0.2	2.5	1.7	6.8	6.6
40–4	0.4	0.4	2.4	1.2	6.5	5.5
45–9	0.4	0.3	2.8	1.4	6.0	4.8
50–4	0.5	0.4	2.8	1.5	6.6	4.5
55–9	1.6	0.7	7.0	3.0	9.8	5.6
60 and over	5.1	4.8	6.4	4.1	6.6	4.2

Note: * Size of enterprise in number of regular employees.
Source: MOL 1988c: 190

integral part of career development and/or as a means of making employment adjustments.

> According to this agency's [Economic Planning Agency] Questionnaire Survey on Corporate Behavior in Fiscal Year 1987, 90 per cent of business enterprises have in the past used personnel from the main line of business by transfer and long-term dispatch to secure the necessary personnel for diversification and moving into new business areas, while 30 per cent of the enterprises have filled their personnel needs through mid-career hiring .... As for the prospects for the next three years, 80 per cent of the companies expect to use outside assignment while 50 per cent expect to use mid-career hiring. While outside assignment will still be dominant, the number of companies that will seek capable people outside the company or enterprise group will be increasing. (EPA 1988: 178)

Japanese companies are reluctant to hire people with previous work experience because of a still widely held presumption that such recruits are temperamentally unstable since they were unable to adjust properly to their previous employer's corporate network of human relations. Because Japanese corporate culture thrives on constant interaction with fellow-employees, the problem of mid-career hiring centres around the integration of the latecomer (Chapter 3). The general rule of thumb seems to indicate that at least two years will be needed for complete integration. The acceptance process is extremely delicate in the case of the new recruit placed in a supervisory position (Chapter 6). In addition, mid-career hiring is generally not accompanied by an increase in salary, which is typical of the long-term approach to employment and remuneration (Chapter 4).

A practice similar to mid-career hiring is the transferring of personnel (*shukkô*) from a large company to a smaller one to which it is usually related (Chapter 8). Reasons for transfer include: employees who reach the age limit, redundant managerial staff, and training. Transfer can be temporary (a period of two to three years) or permanent. The practice has increased rapidly in recent years in order to carry out personnel reduction and/or implement business diversification; on average, 6 per cent of the regular staff in larger companies is active elsewhere with over half of them exercising managerial functions. Among corporations listed on the stock exchanges in 1987 the following percentages practised transfers:

5,000+ employees	91.6 per cent
1,000–4,999	77.0 per cent
300–999 employees	49.4 per cent

Source: MOL 1987a

The transfer rate was particularly high for large firms in depressed industries such as nonferrous metals and chemicals, where workforce reduction has been a necessity.

IN FOREIGN FIRMS

Since the exact number of so-called foreign firms is not known, the number they employ can only be estimated. Perhaps less than 300,000 Japanese are working in companies whose management is controlled or largely controlled by foreign interests. What happens to them should not be considered as representative of what happens to their 40 million counterparts on the domestic labour market. According to MITI, the one thousand or so foreign firms who participated in their surveys employed less than 0.5 per cent of the labour force (MITI 1990c: 141).

For the year 1987, the Ministry of Labour recorded 144,334 regular employees and 5,629 part-time workers in their survey of 990 foreign companies, with 50 per cent or more foreign equity including foreign branches and foreign subsidiaries. Over the span of one year these foreign firms hired 16,591 new employees of whom 8,220 were hired in mid-career but, on the other hand, lost nearly 9,000 (Table 2.6).

The steady increase of foreign firms entering Japan's market or expanding their operations, particularly in the financial industry, is contributing to the recent development, 'that large numbers of science and engineering graduates are turning their backs on the manufacturing industries and entering the financial and insurance sectors. They are drawn by more attractive salaries and the shift in the economy to services and related sectors' (*Nikkeiren* 1990: 10).

The influx of foreign firms has also intensified the demand for skills that to a large extent are independent from the prevalent style of employment (Chapter 3) and nature of corporate organization (Chapter 5). These skills bring in higher salaries than would be the case where expertise is directly determined by the corporate environment. In this sense, mid-career hiring by foreign firms is encouraged. At the same time, however, it seems that along with this type of hiring goes the understanding that the employee is less likely to be

Table 2.6 Foreign firms: number of regular and part-time employees in 1987 and employees recruited and separated in the past year (1986–7)

Industries and foreign capital ratio (number of firms)	Regular employees			Recruited in past year				Separated in past year
	Total	Female	Part-time	Total	Mid-career			
					Number	(per cent)		
Total	(990)	144,334	32,068	5,629	16,591	8,220	56.0	8,966
Construction	(1)	9	1	–	1	1	100.0	1
Manufacturing	(326)	94,132	18,980	2,559	7,883	2,849	48.4	4,101
Wholesale and retail	(431)	30,005	6,539	1,154	4,126	2,543	59.0	2,505
Banking and insurance	(84)	12,226	4,864	582	3,248	1,939	70.1	1,500
Real estate	(2)	15	5	3	8	8	50.0	1
Transport and communications	(31)	2,108	586	171	245	128	39.9	243
Services	(115)	5,839	1,093	1,160	1,080	752	60.3	615
Foreign capital ratio:								
100 per cent	(460)	56,286	15,293	1,786	6,598	3,450	65.3	3,573
More than 50–less than 100 per cent	(155)	20,394	3,407	1,022	2,048	1,030	48.6	1,207
50 per cent	(259)	48,568	7,275	1,824	4,158	1,574	38.8	2,341
Subsidiaries of foreign firms	(36)	6,263	1,158	283	748	380	54.2	389
Branches	(80)	12,823	4,935	714	3,039	1,786	73.5	1,456

Source: MOL 1988b: 61 and 75

concerned about long-term employment security; his readiness to be hired mid-career implies that he would be willing to move to yet another foreign firm.

The hiring of Japanese staff is often mentioned as a major obstacle for foreign firms. A recent example of one foreign company illustrates the time and effort that it requires:

> In FY 1986, Nihon DEC (Digital Equipment Corp.) recruited 208 people at the mid-career level. Here are the results of the recruiting process.
>
> Recruiting results:
>
> | | |
> |---|---:|
> | Applications received | 6,615 |
> | No. interviewed | 1,741 |
> | No. who took written examination | 1,670 |
> | No. selected | 228 |
> | No. who accepted offer | 208 |
>
> Recruitment sources of selected applicants:
>
> | | |
> |---|---:|
> | Advertising* | 139 |
> | Introduced by current employees | 35 |
> | Recruiting firms** | 34 |
> | Previous applicants | 7 |
> | Part-timers now made full-timers | 6 |
> | Japanese students at foreign universities | 7 |
> | Total | 228 |
>
> *Advertising in Asahi, Mainichi, Yomiuri, and Nikkei drew 2,680 applicants of whom 61 received offers. Magazine advertising drew 2,640 applicants of whom 78 received offers.
> **Introduced 780 applicants. Thirteen such firms were responsible for roughly 80 per cent of these introductions and 80 per cent of the 34 who received offers (IIBC 1987: 30).

Contrary to the practice seen in Japanese companies, recruiting graduates regularly is often not a standard activity of foreign firms. Of course, the longer these firms have been active in Japan, the more the practice prevails, but even after a presence of ten or more years, such cases are evident in less than one out of two firms (MOL 1988b: 98). A recent development which may have a significant impact is the fact that very promising female graduates are attracted to the less sex-biased atmosphere of foreign firms. Few firms, however, are enthusiastic about organizing elaborate and lengthy introductory training programs common among their Japanese competitors (Chapter 3).

On the other hand, more than half (56 per cent) of the newly recruited employees are those with previous work experience (see Table 2.6). This is common in international joint ventures, where initial staffing is the responsibility of the Japanese parent company which transfers over the necessary personnel. A temporary transfer of two or three years is usually a necessity in order to bring the new company on stream, but also to give it an image that would help future recruiting. It is then wise to determine a time limit on such transfers since it will be clear to the personnel in the joint-venture that temporary transferees do not bind their fate to that of the new company.

The mid-career hired manager in particular is a common presence in foreign firms. But he can also be a problem. Since obviously not all employees are satisfied with their employment conditions, foreign executives are inclined to be on the look-out for the 'dissatisfied' manager. Among them, usually at the larger domestic companies, are those who may state some willingness to move to a foreign company, but balk at the actual offer. But in foreign firms they are readily approachable. It seems that once a Japanese has changed his employer, to move to yet another foreign employer is easy, but to move back to a Japanese employer is practically out of the question. The offer of a higher salary may trigger a favourable response based on the simple *caveat*: if the offer of a higher salary is what makes the difference, the next offer, still higher, by another foreign firm may be equally the determining factor.

The hiring of a local manager is often decided by the expatriate executive who, under favourable circumstances, could judge the capacities of the new manager, beyond that of having some fluency in the English language. The question is whether the next expatriate, two or three years later, will have the same foresight.

Furthermore, in Japan, the evaluation of managerial performance is not based on short-term criteria (Chapter 6); it needs to be measured by a collective yardstick, namely the blending of individual capacities with corporate culture. Acceptance by peers and subordinates is required. The new manager in the foreign firm may not succeed either because his potential was over-estimated from the start or because of a serious lack of Japanese-like corporate culture into which he can blend, the latter being more often the case. Hence, the practice in a number of foreign firms is to recruit for a few years (*shoku-taku*) a retired Japanese executive, usually in his early sixties, who may be given the position of chairman (*kai-chô*) and who, besides helping the new company to develop the necessary contacts in Japan's business world, is first and foremost entrusted with the task of helping the expatriate executive in recruiting new graduates as well as experienced personnel (Chapter 10).

On the minds of most Japanese employees in foreign firms (which is no doubt on the minds of most Japanese), there is a lingering uncertainty as to the *permanency* in Japan of their current employer. Such uncertainty is more a problem of image than of reality. Many of the foreign firms are newcomers in Japan and have had no time yet to establish an image of permanency. On the other hand, the number of foreign firms ceasing operations in Japan is not small. 'Actual withdrawals and liquidations of wholly foreign-owned subsidiaries in Japan, as reported by the MITI, totaled nine in FY1984, 25 in FY1985 and seven in the first-half of FY1986. If foreign withdrawals from Japan-based joint ventures with Japanese partners are included, the figures are respectively 19 and 40 for FY1984 and FY1985, 14 for first-half FY1986' (IIBC 1987: 8). A further factor of uncertainty is often the fact of merger or acquisition of the parent company to be implemented in its Japanese subsidiaries. Apparently, all this is enough for many young and mature Japanese to hesitate considering employment in a foreign firm.

3 Work and its environment

Temporary and part-time employment are mere buffers which allow the regular workforce to enjoy the benefits of the employment *relationship*, whereby a sort of labour aristocracy is created whose vested interests are also represented by the labour union. *Regular* employment takes a clearly collective approach involving a corporate dimension maintained on complex and long-term dynamics. By starting employment after graduation, young Japanese become *shakai-jin*, fully-fledged members of society, which means they are now expected to contribute to society. The workplace becomes a community of fate (*kyôdô-tai*), and this is highlighted by the fact that members of the industrial society identify themselves with their place of work (*shoku-ba*), contrary to the Western practice where identity is determined by one's skill, occupation, or profession. The popular term for regular employees is not employees but corporate members (*sha-in*). The manager is as much a *sha-in* as the clerk or the production worker. The common denominator is corporate loyalty. In Japan, being employed is not interpreted as having a job, for this would refer to an individual's qualification, but having a place of work, which reflects a collective dimension. The late Konosuke Matsushita, founder of Matsushita Electrical Industrial Co., addressing a group of American and European executives visiting Japan, stated in his usual forceful manner: 'Your "socially-minded bosses", often full of good intentions, believe their duty is to protect the people in their firms. We, on the other hand, are realists and consider it our duty to get our people to defend their firms, which will pay them back a hundredfold for their dedication. By doing this, we end up by being more "social" than you' (as quoted in Trevor 1988: 238).

The long-term employment relationship is often referred to as life-time employment (*shûshin koyô*). Thus, when the Japanese identifies himself in industrial terms by his workplace and not by his occupation, he understands the basic facts of the industrial lifecycle, i.e. birth, ageing and death, in somewhat the following manner.

Birth: Hired by a given company at industrial age zero, i.e. at the time he graduates from school;

Ageing: The merit in years of service (*nenkô*) in that same company;

Death: Termination of the employment relationship at the mandatory age limit (*teinen*).

A perspective such as this changes the individual's fundamental attitude towards industrial work, and consequently the nature of the workplace itself.

One salient characteristic of the large majority of Japanese workers is that they do not regard their jobs simply as a means of earning an income. Instead, they attach a great deal of importance to the intrinsic compensation derived from work itself – for example, from opportunities to use aptitudes and abilities. Belonging to a company can be interpreted more clearly as a sense of belonging to the whole company as a place of employment rather than to any specific job. While the expectation of some intrinsic compensation derived from work remains strong, 'work' does not connote a specific job but encompasses a rather wide range of diverse occupations. This characteristic reflects clearly a situation where (1) labor unions are organized into enterprise-based units in which all employees of individual companies are members, regardless of their occupations or job classifications; (2) especially in the case of white-collar work, corporate organizations typically promote generalized personnel training programs in an effort to avoid specialization of personnel in specific jobs; and (3) there is, as a result, ample flexibility in assignment of personnel to suit the company's particular needs. (Inagami 1988: 25)

The spirit behind regular employment is deep-rooted in the Buddhist maxim of *ichiren takusho*, 'together to paradise on the same lotus petal'. Employment is not determined by a contractual type of relationship (the labour contract), but by a *human* relationship. No contractual *quid pro quo* is necessary; the emphasis is on cooperation (Chapter 8). As can be expected, the company concerns itself with matters well beyond the workplace, including the personal and family matters of the employee. As in the context of family or community, the relationship depends on social values more than mere economic considerations. Promotion, like ranking in the family, progresses along a vertical axis, where one's greater or lesser experience of *life*, i.e. years of service, is the determining factor. In postwar Japan there is not much of a gap – social, ideological or otherwise – between blue- and white-collar employees, and between management and labour.

The Japanese company is grateful to the longevity of its *sha-in*, i.e. for remaining loyal to the firm. The technical term, commonly used in relation to work compensation, is *nenkô* or the merit in the number of years an employee has provided his services. This word is often, and misleadingly, translated as seniority. In essence, it refers to the development of the human resource in the corporate setting, namely the *sha-in*. Inexperienced though he may be about matters concerning the company, the new employee, fresh out of school, is hired for his potential. He is put through on- and off-the-job training that progressively broadens and deepens his work experience (in terms of various skills) while acclimatizing him to his work environment (in terms of his peers and subordinates). Better performance can be expected from longer experience (complemented by training) which is furthermore compensated by better pay.

The merit in accumulating years of employment is, however, not only appreciated in terms of maturing on the job. It also means maturing according to societal norms. In due course, the new employee will get married and have children. These kinds of social needs are an inseparable aspect of aging and are covered by the compensation system (Chapter 4). *Nenkô* is not the numerical device that seniority is often made out to be; it is the fundamental principle, or more explicitly, the reality of human-resource development in both the industrial and the social objective.

However, life implies expiration, which in the employment relationship means the mandatory age limit (*teinen*). A common practice in large- and medium-size firms, the limit was set at age 55. This did not create a problem as long as life-expectancy remained the same. Employees often continued to work beyond the age limit but on a temporary basis at reduced pay (10 to 30 per cent reduction), without further supervisory responsibility. (A promotion to directorship would mean the termination of the standard employment relationship and the separation allowance would be paid out; the Rules of Employment would henceforth not apply.) In the 1960s and 1970s, as life-expectancy rose to over 70 years and labour union pressure grew, the age limit was extended. Today, most firms have set the limit at 60 (JIL 1989: 80). Such an extension requires negotiating with the labour union, which often wants countermeasures taken specifically regarding the separation allowance (Chapter 4). Whenever possible, elderly employees are transferred to related companies and paid their separation allowance.

Employment security is not only an individual concern for it determines secure work environment. The company and its members must be constantly concerned about corporate growth, i.e. expanding its market share (Chapter 9). Thus automation and diversification are not only readily supported but actively encouraged by the workforce. But this requires continuous training and up-grading of skills. In addition, employment security for the regular employee is equated with the growth of his company. Under these conditions, it is not surprising that corporate mergers and acquisitions are, to say the least, especially difficult in Japan.

> It is considered shameful behavior to sell one's own company. Japanese people are group-oriented, and members of the company have a deep sense of identification with their company and find it difficult to integrate as members of other companies. Wages and promotions are determined by length of service to a great extent, so wages of the same profession in different companies are not necessarily the same. The labour unions are organized on a company-wide basis, so unions tend to be against acquisitions. Since companies guarantee lifetime employment, it is not easy to decrease the number of employees after acquisition. These are important reasons for the lower use of acquisitions in Japan. (Kono 1984: 291)

PERSONNEL ADMINISTRATION

As elaborated in the Rules of Employment or Work Rules (*shûgyô kisoku*), personnel administration is entrusted to the Personnel Department (*jinji-bu* or *jinji-ka*). Although the privileges of regular employees are not asserted by law, they become mandatory if included in the Rules of Employment, which must be registered with the local Labour Standards Bureau whenever ten or more workers are employed (non-regular employees are usually excluded). In Japan, the authority behind these rules is seen by experts as deriving mostly from the fact that the rules are regarded 'not as part of the contract of employment but as part of the law of the enterprise which each employee accepts when he joins it. Like society, every organization, if it is not to become anarchic, must have its own laws, and it will generate them spontaneously' (Ohta 1988: 630).

These Rules of Employment represent collective fairness, i.e. the fair treatment of each and every corporate member (*sha-in*). They constitute more of a general but detailed *sha-in* charter than a set of bylaws that are legally binding (as in a labour contract). Despite their detailed itemization (indispensable in the rare case where legal action might be necessary), the Rules are almost never invoked as some guarantee of an individual's vested right. After all, what maintains satisfaction in the work environment is how status is recognized by the individual and those surrounding him. Differentials in the treatment of employees are perceived most sensitively in all aspects of the *sha-in*'s working conditions, except, however, in matters pertaining to work sharing, when it is assumed everybody exerts his 'best effort' (Iwata 1982: 101).

Technically, these Rules view the Personnel Department as a centralized corporate responsibility (Inohara 1990b). The purpose is not to relieve line managers of a difficult responsibility, but to bring about a stronger sense of community and fate for one and all, which is what *regular* employees expect. The employer is not some given supervisor, nor group of executives, but the corporate community as promoted by the Personnel Department which provides more than just clerical administration, offering both objective and subjective inputs that transform work and its environment into a fruitful learning experience.

> [T]he centralization of personnel administration is an important mechanism through which the [Japanese] firm ensures that individual employees will comply with the organizational objective despite the wide-range delegation of decision making to the lower level of the functional hierarchy and nonhierarchical coordination. In short, the centralized administration of the ranking hierarchy complements and substitutes for decentralization in the functional hierarchy in the [Japanese] firm.... The training of employees in a wide range of skills and the practice of rotating personnel between functional units may thus discourage personnel from asserting inefficient sectarian interests in the organization. (Aoki 1988: 286)

The motivation of regular employees is generally high, or at least high enough to make a noticeable difference. Creating motivation to work is practical; it means stimulating a work process that essentially stands for, and results in, quality (Chapter 9). Small-group activities so efficiently used for quality control provide incentives that help to build initiative and increase participation. In the early 1970s, such activities could be found in 40 per cent and, by the 1980s, in over 60 per cent of the companies with 100 or more employees (MOL 1985: 14). In half of the cases, meetings were held during working hours; if not, overtime was usually paid. QC circles (or anything similar to them) are in most instances autonomous groups of five to ten employees that continue a practice every Japanese child learned from kindergarten on: to upgrade the collective and individual competence of those involved by participating and learning to recognize how things are done. Thus the habit of *learning by doing* continued. A circle's results are compared from a competitive point of view with those of other QC circles at shop, company and industry levels. Their greatest contribution to the company is in identifying the causes of each problem, which the operators are better at doing than the technical staff; the latter are more involved in the solution.

Besides its economic contribution to quality assurance, the Just-in-Time or *kanban* system is effective in cultivating the participation of operators in the flow of work.

> The *kanban* system emphasizes the efficient utilization of manpower rather than the full utilization of machines, the result of which may be unneeded accumulations of in-process inventories. Multifunctional workers are also more effective in operating the multipurpose numerical-control machines that are replacing single-purpose machines as the emphasis shifts from economies of scale to repeated short-production runs of similar parts with short lead times. When the demand from the downstream shop slackens, idle workers are deployed in the maintenance of machines and other household jobs of the shop. Further, workers trained in a wide range of skills can better understand why more defective products are being produced and how to cope with the situation as well as prevent it from recurring. If horizontal coordination is to operate smoothly, product defects must be spotted in advance of the final inspection, namely, at the very place where the problem occurs, and remedial measures must be taken immediately. (Aoki 1988: 36-7)

Consequently, labour productivity keeps increasing. With 1985=100 as the base, productivity was 95.8 in 1984, 101.8 in 1986, 107.6 in 1987, 119.4 in 1988 and 127.0 in 1989 (Statistics Bureau 1990: 113). It would, however, be erroneous to conclude that an individual's work satisfaction would also be higher. In fact, it was not (Komai 1989: chapter 3; Kono 1984: 332). Apparently, this contradiction addresses the problem of satisfaction being a function of expectation. *Sha-in* have much greater expectations about their work

Table 3.1 International comparison of working hours

	1986		1987	
	Hours worked (overtime)			
Japan	2,150	(212)	2,168	(224)
US	1,924	(177)	1,949	(192)
UK	1,938	(161)	1,947	(177)
FDR	1,655	(83)	1,642	(78)
France	1,643	(–)	1,645	(–)

Source: JETRO 1990: 124

environment than employees elsewhere; under these circumstances, satisfaction of their expectations is also more difficult to attain. None the less, Japanese employees are often described as workaholics. As a matter of fact, it is not that the Japanese are working *hard* but rather that they work *long*, motivation being provided not by the work, but by the work environment. An international comparison of working hours in 1986 and 1987, based on estimates given for workers in the manufacturing and production industries, reached the conclusion shown in Table 3.1.

ORGANIZED LABOUR

The postwar Constitution of Japan (1946), under Article 28, granted the following three 'Labour Rights': to organize, to bargain collectively, and to act collectively (popularly understood as the right to strike). Soon afterwards, some legal restrictions were added to these rights. In the public sector, national and local government employees were given the right only to organize and public corporation and national enterprise employees were given the rights only to organize and bargain collectively. For decades, these restrictions remained a source of discord in the labour movement. Not surprisingly, in 1988, there were 1.4 million union members in the public sector, and their rate of unionizing was over 70 per cent. The main obstacle to the unification of the labour movement had been the rivalry between the unions in the public sector, who were more inclined to radicalism, and the more moderate unions in the large private companies. Unification of some sort was finally achieved in 1989 after 30 years of bickering.

Most industries have a so-called industrial union (*tansan*) which is

Table 3.2 Number of labour unions, membership and estimated rate of organization, 1970–89

Year (as of 30 June)	Number of unions	Membership (1,000)	Organization rate (est.)
Total 1970	30,058	11,605	35.4
1980	34,232	12,369	30.8
1985	34,539	12,418	28.9
1986	34,216	12,343	28.2
1987	34,033	12,272	27.6
1988	33,750	12,277	26.8
1989	33,683	12,227	25.9

Source: MOL 1990a: 13, 27–8

an industry-wide federation of labour unions. Such loose organizations play a coordinating role, particularly in staging the *shuntô* (spring wage offensive), where some play the role of pace-setters in negotiating wage increases. Most do not, however, intervene directly in collective bargaining at the enterprise level and their directives do not bind affiliated unions.

The postwar rate of unionizing increased steadily until the end of the 1960s and started to decline: in 1970 to 35.4 per cent, in 1980 to 30.8 per cent, and in 1989 to 26.8 per cent or 12.2 million union members (Table 3.2). In comparison, this rate was 46.9 per cent in the UK (1987), 40.9 per cent in West Germany (1988) and 16.8 per

Table 3.3 Number of labour unions, membership and estimated rate of organization by selected industries, 1988 and 1989

Selected industries	Number of unions		Membership (1,000)		Organization rate (est.)	
	1988	1989	1988	1989	1988	1989
Manufacturing	11,425	11,343	4,045	4,026	32.6	30.9
Transportation and communications	4,900	4,906	1,755	1,708	57.4	50.1
Wholesale and retail	2,967	3,008	900	923	8.8	9.0
Finance and insurance, real estate	1,066	1,079	1,089	1,122	50.0	49.9
Services	8,336	8,310	1,698	1,709	16.3	15.5

Source: MOL 1990a: 27–8

cent in the US (1989) (Keizai Koho Center 1991: 73). The decline in union membership is probably, as in the case of other industrial countries, due to the shift from blue-collar to white-collar employment and the concomitant shift from secondary- to tertiary-sector employment (Table 3.3). This is particularly visible in areas that had traditionally been centres of union strength, such as steel, shipbuilding and electrical machinery. National labour centres struggle to reverse the trend, but with little success.

Concerning the individual company, the typical form of labour organization (used by over 80 per cent) is the enterprise union (*kigyô-betsu kumiai*); this union negotiates directly with their company's management, excluding outsiders (such as the industry-wide federation or national labour centre). Its membership is limited to the regular employees of the enterprise; temporary and part-time employees, as well as employees of subcontractors working on the premises, are excluded as a rule. The union makes little, if any, distinction between blue- and white-collar or technical and clerical employees. Among supervisory staff, the dividing line is usually drawn, in small firms, at the level of *ka-chô* (section chief), and in large firms, at the level of *kakari-chô* (sub-section chief). The standard is thus 'one company, one union'. But an enterprise union is not normally a company union, i.e. dominated by the management. It feels equally qualified to speak about the company as management without, however, truly questioning management prerogatives, because an end to the company means the end of the enterprise union. The function of an enterprise union is, ultimately, to protect regular employment, namely the *norm* based on lifetime employment (which is conditional on the survival of the enterprise).

Each side of labour–management relations has, of course, different interests. In most industrial countries the interests are not only different, they are also perceived as *divergent* (expressed by the equation $1 + 1 = 2$). Generally speaking, labour and management in Japan do have different interests, but corporate culture tends to make them *converge* (like the two sides of a coin; each is different but the reality is in the coin itself: $1 \times 1 = 1$). Hence two broad characteristics of Japanese-type labour–management relations stand out. One is institutional, where the relationship is to a large extent internalized, i.e. the company is the *raison d'être* of management and labour, be it organized or not. The other characteristic is psychological; the relationship easily turns emotional, i.e. internalization fosters a high dose of subjectivity. In Western economies, organizing the worker is essentially in the form of a *trade* union (for the individual identifies himself with his trade or occupation); in Japan, at least in postwar years, the so-called *enterprise* union is the norm (for the individual identifies himself with his place of work).

The officers of an enterprise union are regular employees of the firm who remain on the payroll during their term of office, usually for a year. They are nominated by out-going officers and elected by all members. Under normal circumstances, these officers have a major role as informal intermediaries between management and union. They then become considered as good managerial potential. In 1978 and 1981 the Japan Federation of Employers' Associations surveyed more than 300 large companies, about half of which were in manufacturing. Among their 6,000 or so directors, over 15 per cent were former union officers (*Nikkeiren* 1981: 25).

LABOUR–MANAGEMENT RELATIONS

The major activity involving labour unions is collective bargaining (*dantai kôshô*). The collective agreement (*dantai kyôyaku*) which results from it, however, is not much more than a formality which recognizes the labour union; it repeats at length whatever legal provisions exist and the company's Rules of Employment, in addition to some provisions about qualification for union membership, etc. Union security is usually maintained by a union-shop clause. Collective bargaining, it should be noted, is not limited to the period of the collective agreement; it takes place at *shuntô*, the time for wage increases, and any time during the year when it concerns other working conditions. Grievance procedures are often specifically noted in the collective agreement but hardly ever used.

In the standard of 'one company, one union', there is no jurisdictional conflict among unions. Exceptional is the case where a 'second union' (*daini kumiai*) is formed, usually at the instigation of management after the original union antagonized some employees with its overly zealous actions. This is a rare instance in Japanese companies, but wherever it is found it creates protracted labour unrest.

Labour disputes have reflected a different situation in public and private sectors. In the former, a perennial issue has been the right to strike; as late as the 1970s the more aggressive public unions staged strikes in order to obtain the right to strike! In the private sector, where the survival of the labour union depends directly on the survival of the enterprise it organizes, disputes that often flared in bloody clashes in the 1950s have simmered down to short work stoppages, usually to express support for the current spring wage offensive.

Over half of the officially recorded disputes occur in firms with less than 300 employees (MOL 1989f: 26). As is often the case, labour unrest stops short of carrying out work stoppage that may damage the enterprise, particularly in smaller enterprises; noisy demonstrations are held during lunch breaks or after working hours. Labour unrest climaxing in halting the normal flow of work

> has become symbolic of a total breakdown in the relationship of trust between employer and the union, and it is not unknown for employers to top up an offer in order to avoid a strike. Labour and management share the view that the real and psychological blows dealt to a firm by a strike seriously threaten its viability. Both are motivated therefore, and inclined to solve problems through exhaustive discussions. (Takanashi 1989: 22)

Current legislation protects labour unilaterally, but the judicial process is not much appreciated as such and is often regarded by labour unions as one more reason to demonstrate against the employer. In fact, legalities seem ill-suited when what is at stake is not so much a contract under which a dispute could be settled by the application of legal or universal principles but a relationship whose constant dynamics have to be negotiated and where only particulars apply.

Labour courts do not exist in Japan. Any complaint of unfair labour practice is submitted to the civil courts, usually by the individual. Local and Central Labour Relations Commissions established after World War II permit a worker or a labour union to submit complaints about unfair labour practices or seek intervention in a labour dispute. Arbitration is rarely called for; almost all cases are handled by conciliation and only a few by mediation. Whereas the civil court judges the case from a strictly legal viewpoint, the Commission reaches a conclusion from a more flexible administration of redress. 'The average length of the period of the procedures at both Local and Central Labour Commissions in the last few years have ranged from about 500 days to 800 days.... [U]nions which brought cases to the Commission often found merit in keeping the proceedings going for as long as possible, if not forever' (Hanami 1983: 7). Parties not satisfied with the Commission's orders may bring the case to civil court.

Labour–management relations are not limited to collective bargaining. In the mid-1950s joint councils (*rôshi kyôgikai*) started to be promoted as a part of the productivity movement and are now found in over 90 per cent of Japanese enterprises, often established

Table 3.4 Comparison of the two types of formal labour–management interaction

Features	Collective bargaining	Joint consultation
Character	Clash of interests	Common interests
Contents	Labour conditions (negotiations)	Production increase (cooperation)
Objective	Sharing of fruits	Enlargement of resources for sharing
Effectiveness of results	Binding forces	Flexibility

Source: Japan Productivity Center 1982

by the collective labour agreement. Whereas collective bargaining implies a situation of confrontation to be resolved by compromise, joint consultation with the union or others representing personnel is looked upon as a peaceful and reasonable attempt at reaching an understanding through open communication. Joint consultation is usually regarded as a preliminary step leading to collective bargaining. In large companies, joint councils are especially active at the local level (in branches and plants). Table 3.4 shows how the Japan Productivity Center (1982) describes the respective features of the two types of formal labour–management interaction.

In small/medium enterprises, unions are not very effective in terms of settling wages but are somewhat more successful with the issue of benefits, both monetary and non-monetary, and in dealing with on-the-job training. In addition to a labour union, or substituting for it, an employee association (*sha-in-kai*) is commonly found in these firms. According to a 1988 survey of small and medium enterprises, employee associations were found in the unionized sector in 43.2 per cent of the manufacturing firms and 45.4 per cent of the service firms; in the non-unionized sector they were found in 72 per cent of the manufacturing and 65 per cent of the service firms (Osawa 1989: 7). Compared to labour unions, employee associations have a greater flexibility in membership criteria; while the labour union limits its membership to regular employees, the employee association can include managers and even temporary workers. Representatives are usually elected and often are managers. The association may legally engage in collective bargaining but it cannot negotiate a collective labour agreement.

IN FOREIGN FIRMS

Foreign firms active in Japan face serious difficulties in meeting the expectations of the workforce they employ. Since the *sha-in* (corporate members) expect fairness and security of working conditions not from a contract but from a relationship, a constant concern of the Japanese employee in the foreign firm is the permanency of the firm in Japan. The foreign firm does not offer the same *permanency* that large Japanese firms do, since the home office is considered a remote entity with its own dynamics, and expatriate managers are frequently rotated. More telling is the little-justified 'feeling' that top management, especially the position of company president, is a foreign preserve (Chapter 6). Generally, the fundamental criterion of years of service is given much less importance. What emerges is an implicit threat to employment security, or to any enterprise union that aims to ensure such security.

A recent development largely due to the influx of foreign firms should be noted: the multiplication of financial institutions and R&D centres has encouraged proposals for new types of skill requirements, sometimes referred to as 'professional manpower' by the Japanese. The view here is that some financial specialists and some scientists are largely interchangeable among companies, in the sense that the skill they exercise is hardly, if at all, determined by a specific corporate context. A limited number of Japanese, often trained abroad, have jumped on the bandwagon. But this kind of job situation is understood by their less enthusiastic countrymen as having higher pay without having the accustomed security.

What is also often neglected in foreign firms is the learning environment, and thus the growth of the individual is in a way stunted for the lack of such an environment, which evolves from a corporate policy with objectives that go beyond profit. As a result, Japanese

Table 3.5 Comparison of Japanese and foreign firms' facilitation of internal communication

	Japanese firms (1984)	Foreign firms (1987)
Workshop meetings	77.7 per cent	44.1 per cent
Small-group activities	60.2 per cent	43.2 per cent

Source: MOL 1985: 13–17, and MOL 1988b: 33

employees in foreign firms look for that extra something: higher salaries, rapid promotion or even another foreign firm.

Foreign firms trail behind their Japanese competitors in facilitating internal communication, particularly regarding workshop meetings and small-group activities. The percentage of foreign firms sponsoring such activities is substantially less than that of their local competitors, as is shown in Table 3.5.

Currently, only 15 per cent of foreign firms have a labour union; it seems that the larger the ratio of Japanese capital, the greater the likelihood of a union. As would be the case in local industry, the smaller the size of the firm, the less the chances are that a union would be organized. Where they do exist, a majority of the employees are members (MOL 1988b: 78). The creation of a labour union is mostly a manifestation of insecurity in the question of employment (sudden dismissal, neglect of standard procedures, etc.). Although, these days, a rather rare instance for the Japanese firm, the union has been known to take an aggressive stand, often with the support of outside labour organizers, when, justifiably or not, it feels that its *raison d'être* or employment security is threatened. In many cases, this state of agitation takes months, if not years, to calm down.

Two major weak points of foreign firms are that, contrary to their local competitors, first, their Japanese managers often lack labour union experience and, second, the Personnel Department, if it exists, is not expected to cultivate informal contacts with union officers and is not actively involved in developing or enhancing labour–management communication. In the case of dispute, the tendency of the expatriate executives is then to entrust the problem to *outsiders*, of whom the least qualified are often the labour experts at the home office. Consequently, the union feels entitled to bringing in its own outsiders. In Japan, a labour lawyer may be retained for advice but he is not used for actual negotiations, which should remain an internal matter.

It could well be that inexperience about labour relations in Japan is the reason why plural unionism is not uncommon in unionized foreign firms: in 1987, some 20 out of 156 organized foreign companies had to deal with more than one labour union (MOL 1988b: 78). These are usually cases involving Labour Relations Commissions and the courts over an extended period. 'Employers, eventually, are inclined to get involved in such interunion conflicts. Some of these plural union cases which are particularly difficult to handle are related to discrimination in promotion and wage increases based on performance evaluation.... In many of the local Commissions the average length of procedures for such cases reaches more than 1,000 days' (Hanami 1983: 8).

A joint labour–management council is found in 59.1 per cent of the foreign firms with more than 100 employees (72 per cent in Japanese firms of similar size); on the average, the number of sessions held per year is 6.4, as against 15.6 in Japanese firms (MOL 1985: 10, and MOL 1988b: 89). The number of employee associations is even fewer. Management indifference in this regard may be reflected by an equal indifference on the part of the Japanese workforce: if work satisfaction is low, the move to another foreign firm is made all the more easier.

In sum, a considerable amount of time and energy must be applied to labour–management relations in foreign firms, exactly as the Japanese competitors do. Collective bargaining can be requested by the labour union at any time, while the same could be expected with a joint council. In fact, long sessions are interpreted as a demonstration of management *sincerity* in discussing or negotiating with the work-force. (In addition, any formal session requires other informal preparatory discussions, as will be noted in Chapter 7.) Foreign exec-utives, whose time and energy are already largely absorbed by communicating with the home office, are reluctant to spend time in collective bargaining. Their Japanese colleagues, most of whom are inexperienced in these matters, would prefer to remain in the side-lines. In Japan, this is all part of the subjectivity that shapes and moulds the reality of the human experience in the workplace.

Part II

The workplace

The employment relationship, at least for regular employees, is taken from the long-term perspective. From this point of view, labour in Japanese companies is a fixed cost requiring careful management to insure that, first, payroll obligations are met, and, second, motivation is sustained among the regular workforce. Work compensation is a component in an altogether complex yet balanced system where the 'merit in years of service' is given precedence. An organic style of corporate organization is what evolves, emphasizing the work process rather than the fruits which result from it. The role of the manager becomes more of a coordinator than a supervisor. Furthermore, personnel management is centralized, which allows for a substantial decentralization of the decision-making process.

Executives and managers in foreign firms, be they Japanese or expatriate, often find themselves trapped by the pressure of fulfilling short-term objectives to satisfy the home office, if not also by expectations that they themselves have set. Results pursued in this way can be detrimental to the long-term performance, especially when human relations within and outside the enterprise are neglected. Efficiency is desired, but the foreign firm may be lacking the elements which make it effective.

4 Work compensation

The Japanese competitor considers human resources as his primary asset. Focus is placed not so much on managing as *developing* it according to its long-term potential. As noted in Part 1, the basis of the employment relationship for the *sha-in* is not a contractual *quid pro quo* but a quasi-permanent relationship, where compensation is clearly a long-term proposition. The Rules of Employment explain the salary system in detail, making it clear to all corporate members that employment is a long-term corporate investment. Differentials in individual salaries are justified and accepted only against this system.

In Japan, blue-collar as well as white-collar employees are paid by the month. In official statistics, monthly salaries for regular employees are referred to as scheduled cash earnings (*shotei-nai kyûyo*), which includes the basic salary and various monthly allowances excluding overtime pay. But monthly earnings alone comprises only two-thirds or less of the annual income from work, the difference being compensated by seasonally paid allowances. In addition, another payment is given out upon leaving the company which might amount to the equivalent of at least a month's worth of earnings for each year of service.

The *sha-in* thus receives a kind of life income distributed in the form of a monthly salary and other benefits. Graphically speaking, salary can be expressed as some point on a positive curve which extends over a period of 30 years or so. One basic characteristic of this curve is that salary steadily rises over the years of service by a few thousand yen each year. This curve is not only determined by corporate personnel policy but also by a combination of factors including educational background, length of service and work performance. From its 1987 'Model Wages' derived from the annual wage survey of large companies, the Central Labour Relations Commission calculated how much more the male *sha-in* would earn at age 55, in comparison to what he earns at age 22:

- White-collar
    College graduate   3.82 times
    High school graduate   3.16 times
- Blue-collar
    High school graduate   2.63 times
    Junior high school graduate   2.52 times
    (MOL 1988h: 9)

Although, as will later be described in further detail, the salary *system* is fairly uniform among companies of comparable size, actual individual amounts are not. No standard market rates are given beyond starting salaries of new graduates. Average salaries themselves must be viewed with caution, since companies tend to define the various employee qualifications in the system differently, and wide variations exist according to industry, size of enterprise, average age of the workforce and ratio of female employees.

> The large-firm sector usually recruits employees from new graduates and promotes them within the internal labour market of the firm. The small-firm sector depends more on family workers, retired people from large firms, and part-time workers or housewives. Some argue that wage differentials reflect merely quality differences of workers in the two sectors, but this sounds sweeping, if partly true. When the labour market is slack, wage differentials tend to be larger as large firms cannot decrease wage rates but can only slightly reduce the number of employees for the sake of keeping the cooperative relationship with the company labour union, whereas wage rates are more downwardly flexible to small firms as labour fixedness is much lower. (Sekiguchi 1986: 256)

STARTING SALARIES

Given the concern for the average age of the corporate workforce and consequently the concern for hiring graduates straight from school (Chapter 2), the starting salary offered to the newly recruited graduate is an indication of labour-market conditions. Because of the keen competition among firms anxious to hire graduates straight from school, the starting salary is the only instance where salary is affected by market rate. Unions do not make it an issue in their wage-increase demands. Differentials in starting salaries by size of the firm cannot be too great because small firms must try to match the initial offer of the larger companies if they want to attract good candidates (a few years after employment, however, a salary gap will emerge and grow). The starting salary is not what attracts the new graduate to a particular employer; attractiveness is measured by the student's perception of what relative importance and lifetime prospects other competing employers offer.

Starting (monthly) salaries for new graduates have increased rapidly over the years. At the end of the 1970s it was ¥100,000 for university graduates; by the end of the 1980s it was more than ¥150,000. Several differentials are at work, the largest being education, which is also an age differential. For example, in 1989, the starting salaries of new graduates were (in thousands of yen):

		Male	Female
University (age 22):	Office work	158	153
	Technical work	161	160
Junior college (age 20):	Office work	137	132
	Technical work	139	134
Senior high school (age 18):	Office work	126	120
	Technical work	125	119

(JETRO 1990: 120)

The company regards each starting salary as a long-term liability added to the payroll. Reporting on this liability, the Ministry of Labour estimated that between 1977 and 1987, in manufacturing, for each additional male *sha-in* at age 60, the cumulative monthly salary, excluding overtime pay and seasonal and separation allowances, would have been as follows:

High school graduates:	in 1977	¥101,684,400
	in 1982	¥128,935,200
	in 1987	¥142,782,000
University graduates:	in 1977	¥124,077,600
	in 1982	¥151,158,000
	in 1987	¥167,059,200

(MOL 1988d: References 46–7)

On the other hand, the starting salary of the mid-career recruit is an entirely different matter. In principle, his salary will be less than what he received from his previous place of employment, and the older the employee is the larger the discrepancy will be. For example, in 1987, in large manufacturing companies the remuneration of a mid-career recruit (university male graduate) aged 35 was 99.1 per cent of the earnings of a regular employee of the same age; at age 45, the ratio was 93.7 per cent, and at age 50, 92.1 per cent. In small firms, the ratio declined to 91.2 per cent, 89.8 per cent and 89.3 per cent respectively. The life earnings of the male employee who changed his employer at the age of 45 was estimated to be reduced by about 15 per cent. Furthermore, it was estimated that in 1986 only about 12 per cent of those who resigned did so for a higher salary (MOL 1988d: 195–9).

Exceptions, notably in the financial industry, can be found where the salary of the newly hired financial genius may be substantially higher, but at the same time it is clearly understood that security is not part of the deal. From this position it is questionable whether or not the higher salary that attracted the new manager in the first place will also be effective in retaining him (Chapter 6).

SALARY COMPONENTS

Four components define the salary system: two make out monthly earnings – the basic salary and monthly allowances – and two deferred payments – seasonal allowances and the separation allowance.

Monthly basic salary

The basic salary (*kihon-kyû*) is thus called because it serves as a base for calculating other major components of the salary system, i.e. for several (not all) of the monthly allowances the largest part of the seasonal allowances, and the entire separation allowance. The basic salary is defined as follows:

1 Usually, it is the major portion, about 80 per cent or more, of monthly earnings (*gekkyû*); in some companies however, it is only half. This is because certain considerations determining the basic salary (e.g. work performance) in some companies are handled under monthly allowances in others.

2 Several differentials are taken into consideration in setting the basic salary, particularly the level of formal education (also an age differential) and sex. Explicit attention is given to individual performance, not on a short-term but on a long-term basis.

3 It increases almost automatically at more or less regular intervals, usually every 12 months, generally at a rate of about 2 per cent at the minimum. This reflects the 'merit in years of service' (*nenkô*), but in practice it is associated with age since it does relate to the social needs of the employee's livelihood which change with time.

Figure 4.1 Theoretical curve of the basic salary

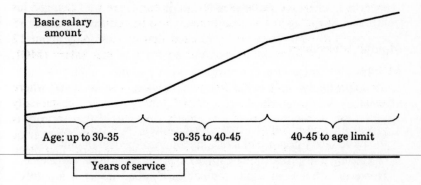

Only in an extreme case would the company defer this increase, perhaps postponing it for a year or a few months.

In graphic form, the basic salary follows a positive curve whose slope varies (see Figure 4.1). In very broad terms, three periods could be distinguished, each corresponding to a specific span in the life of the regular employee:

- Until age 30–5, the incremental rate is slow. Employees are not yet, or only recently, married and their livelihood needs are relatively light. Labour market pressure keeps pushing up the starting salary.
- Between ages 30–5 and 40–5, the rate picks up considerably. Family obligations are heavy.
- After age 40–5, the rate slows down again as needs tend to level off.

The way the basic salary is assigned may vary greatly from company to company. In some companies, amounts are decided within set ranges; in others, a graded system is used. Amounts are usually calculated from one or more salary tables. The regular employee thus knows more or less what to expect for his/her salary years from now. The majority of private companies use a single salary table for the entire regular workforce. Each company, however, has its own tables, making a comparison of companies practically impossible. The most typical, and elaborate, examples are the tables applied to civil servants, where different basic salary tables cover various employment categories such as universities, hospitals, laboratories, maritime services, etc., and each table covers a large number of employees.

(See Koh 1989: 219–27.) As a helpful example the salary table of government administrative staff (230,000 employees) is presented in Appendix I, where its mechanism is described.

Monthly allowances

Monthly allowances (*teate*) contribute greatly to the complexity and, more importantly, to the flexibility of the salary system. Monthly allowances can be described as:

1 Given for considerations that either cannot be incorporated into the basic salary because of a risk in jeopardizing overall uniformity, or causing a disproportionate increase in the separation allowance. However, what is in some companies handled under a monthly allowance may in others be a determinant of basic salary, while there are others who may take both views.
2 On average constituting about 20 per cent or less of monthly earnings (the remainder being the basic salary) excluding overtime pay. Allowances are expressed in specific amounts or ranges of amounts, without direct reference to basic salary.
3 Being of several different types as provided by the Rules of Employment. In addition, statutory contributions to social security

Table 4.1 Monthly supervisory allowances, 1986–9 (in yen)

Monthly supervisory allowance		1986	1987	1988	1989
Fixed amount for all:					
Department head		58,200	54,100	57,300	63,200
Assistant department head		48,800	45,800	47,500	53,600
Section chief		38,000	37,900	36,600	42,800
Deputy section chief		27,200	23,900	25,100	27,100
Amount range:					
Department head	Minimum	76,900	73,100	82,900	80,000
	Maximum	96,200	90,400	102,900	100,200
Assistant dep. head	Minimum	63,500	58,700	64,800	66,000
	Maximum	78,000	72,100	83,200	82,800
Section chief	Minimum	49,600	47,000	52,200	53,200
	Maximum	63,300	60,200	66,700	65,900
Deputy section chief	Minimum	35,400	38,200	40,400	37,300
	Maximum	45,400	51,100	52,100	49,000

Source: CLRC 1989b: 34–5 and previous years

(health, welfare-pension, unemployment, and workmen's accident compensation) are included.

Managerial promotion is not fully recognized under the basic salary, since this would affect the separation allowance in later years; instead this is explicitly covered under the so-called supervisory allowance (Table 4.1). Other allowances are given for attendance or skill; blue-collar employees are eligible for special duty or shift allowance. In addition, allowances related to 'living costs', such as family, housing, or special hardship allowance (e.g. heating costs are higher in Hokkaido) are provided in most cases. Commonly, the cost of commuting from home to work is refunded.

Overtime, paid by the month, is mainly used to help the company adjust to the business cycle. The minimum legal premium is 25 per cent of the hourly wage. Overtime pay often adds up to 10 per cent of monthly earnings. Managers, however, are rarely paid overtime, which is one of the reasons why the supervisory allowance is given.

Seasonal allowances

Although commonly called a *bonus*, the seasonal allowance (*kimatsu teate* in the public sector, *shôyo* in the private sector) is a deferred

Table 4.2 Average separation allowance by education after 30 years of service in large and small firms, 1980–9 (in yen)

Education	Large firms (1,000 or more employees)			
	1981	1985	1987	1989
Middle school	8,900,000	10,155,000	10,772,000	10,647,000
High school	12,800,000	14,100,000	14,430,000	14,707,000
College	18,600,000	19,988,000	20,204,000	20,664,000
Education	Small firms in Tokyo			
	1980	1984	1987	1988
Middle school	5,100,000	6,736,000	7,357,000	6,234,000
High school	6,300,000	8,239,000	8,285,000	8,304,000
College	8,200,000	9,592,000	10,394,000	10,097,000

Sources: CLRC 1989a and previous years; Tokyo Municipal Government 1988 and previous years

wage payment and not exactly a premium. (The director's bonus is a separate matter, since it is treated differently in terms of taxes.) These allowances reflect current corporate performance only to some extent, as they are considered with more flexibility in times of upward corporate growth. In the 1960s, a period of high economic growth, an econometric model determined that 20 per cent of the annual total of seasonal allowances in large companies could be justified by the firm's current net profits and the remaining 80 per cent by the previous year's rate of seasonal allowance (MOL 1973: 21). When a company experiences financial difficulties a reduction or elimination of overtime pay is first carried out; then the seasonal allowance is reduced or postponed if necessary, starting with managers (including the bonus given to executives). This is often a more critical situation in small firms.

The seasonal allowance is:

1 Almost never referred to in specific yen amounts (except for statistical purposes) but as '*X* number of months', for example 2.5 *months*. One such *month* does include the basic salary but only some monthly allowances. Each company has its own method for calculating this figure; thus, *months* and, *a fortiori*, yen amounts can hardly be compared from company to company. Any increase in basic salary will be reflected in the amount of seasonal allowance, but not, of course, in the number of *months*. When a labour union is involved the average number of *months* is usually negotiated, most times without referring to specific amounts.

2 Annually, depending on the company and the type of industry, equal to one-third to one-half of the annual income. Its amount is partly determined, often some 5–10 per cent of it, by work performance (often times, commissions to sales people are paid in the form of a seasonal allowance).

3 Customarily paid on 10 June (the 'summer bonus') and 10 December (the 'winter bonus'); the latter being 10–20 per cent more than the former. (In the public sector a third payment is made at the end of the fiscal year in March.)

Separation allowance

Whenever the employment relationship comes to an end, the regular employee can expect to receive another deferred wage payment not by law but by custom (as stated in the Rules of Employment). This is the separation allowance (*taishoku-kin*) often also translated as retirement allowance. One is disqualified from receiving this allowance if the employee is dismissed for committing some major misdemeanor, or quits during the first or second year of employment. As might be expected, separation allowances are substantially higher in larger than in smaller firms (Table 4.2).

The separation allowance can be described as follows:

1 Separation is distinguished as either resulting from personal reasons (*jiko-tsugô*) or company reasons (*kaisha-tsugô*); this distinction is made clear for tax purposes and other reasons. The former is voluntary; separation is taken as the employee's initiative (better opportunity elsewhere, family reasons, etc.). The amount given in this case is less than that given for corporate reasons, the gap between them narrowing after about 20 years of service. Of the total number of separations in large firms, those resulting from personal reasons were 78.9 per cent in 1970, declining to 73.5 per cent in 1989 (MOL 1990b: 360). Involuntary separation results from the employee's death, some occupational disability, or upon company initiative, i.e. reaching the mandatory age limit (*teinen*) as determined by the norm of lifetime employment, as well as being promoted to the board of directors, corporate bankruptcy, etc.

2 The separation allowance is computed by taking the *basic* salary of the month in which the separation is to take place and multiplying it by a progressive rate, depending on the years of service. This is usually done according to a table providing the coefficients which correspond to the number of years of service. Such a method is standard practice in 90 per cent of the companies and applies to all regular employees regardless of sex or occupational classification (JIL 1989: 79). Merit assessment is not directly furnished, but the last month's basic salary does represent the cumulative achievement of an employee's career.

3 The allowance is usually paid in the form of a lump sum. But a growing number of companies have established a 'qualified' pension plan which includes tax benefits in covering the separation cost (Murakami 1988). The beneficiary is given the option of choosing, under certain conditions, between payment in a lump sum or in annuities; the lump sum is almost always preferred because of its tax advantages.

FLEXIBILITY IN THE SYSTEM

The salary system for regular employees based on the above-mentioned four components – (monthly) basic salary, monthly allowances, seasonal allowances and separation allowance – is indeed complex. But it is in fact from this complexity that the system draws its main advantages. It allows the flexibility necessary to accommodate the individual and the collective dimension of the Japanese workplace as well as the business cycle. Adjustment to short-term business fluctuations is made possible because of overtime and, in some ways, by the seasonal allowances. Long-term adjustment is administered in two ways, the *base-up* and making changes in the retirement system.

Base-up

The popular expression used in annual salary increase negotiations is *base-up*. It reflects the general increase in cost of living and improvement of standards of living, and is implemented at the beginning of the fiscal year, i.e. 1 April, at the time of the Spring Wage Offensive (*shuntô*). Salaries are then raised by a few percentage points: in large companies they rose by 7.68 per cent (¥14,037) in 1980, 5.03 per cent (¥10,871) in 1985, and 5.94 per cent (¥15,026) in 1990 (Keizai Koho Center 1991: 69). These national averages do not reveal the complexities at work behind the standard salary system in the light of

Table 4.3 Rate of salary increase, automatic and negotiated, 1975–89 (per cent)

	Union members			Managerial personnel		
	Total	Automatic	Negotiated	Total	Automatic	Negotiated
1975	14.5	2.0	12.5	12.5	1.7	10.3
1980	7.3	1.6	5.7	7.0	1.2	5.8
1985	5.3	2.4	2.9	4.9	2.1	2.8
1987	3.7	2.3	1.4	3.5	2.1	1.4
1988	4.5	2.2	2.3	4.1	1.9	2.2
1989	5.4	2.3	3.1	5.0	2.1	2.9
1990	6.2	3.7	2.5	5.8	2.3	3.5

Note: 'Negotiated' for managerial personnel means the portion resulting from the revision of the salary table, or influenced by union negotiations.
Source: *Nikkeiren* 1990b: 7 and 9

the conditions relating solely to the firm and the industry. In companies, the *base-up* process could be outlined in the following two steps. First, the enterprise union negotiates the *base-up* for its members to settle on an average percentage. It may specify as benchmarks a certain amount for a given age/sex, e.g. male aged 33. Second, the company applies the *base-up* to all regular employees, including managers, by an equitable distribution over monthly earnings (Table 4.3). A part of the *base-up* is allocated to the basic salary – including the annual automatic increase as well as the updated starting salary (in other words, the basic salary table is revised). The remainder is allocated to monthly allowances; for example, increase of the family and/or cost-of-living allowance, etc.

Of course, when the basic salary changes it affects the seasonal allowances and, most importantly, the separation allowance. Thus, rarely will the entire *base-up* be incorporated in the basic salary, because of the very impact it would have on the separation allowance.

Retirement

The other major adjustment in the salary system concerns the separation allowance, set according to the mandatory age limit under the pressure of a rapidly aging workforce. The age limit is 60 (rarely more) in almost all large companies and in many smaller firms (JIL 1989: 80). Extension of the age-limit would increase the separation allowance, unless countermeasures are negotiated with the labour union (Table 4.4). Generally speaking,

1 The years of service after age 55 (the common age limit until the 1970s) are not counted in the calculation of the separation allowance;
2 From a certain age, say 55, the salary no longer increases; it may even start to decrease;
3 Earlier retirement, for example after the age of 45 and with at least 15 years of service, is encouraged by adding a premium to the separation allowance – for instance, in an amount equivalent to what would be received had they retired at the age of 55; in some companies, this may be a case affecting managers in particular.

INCOME FROM EMPLOYMENT

The distinction between monthly earnings and deferred payments can be emphasized by taking into account how earned income is put to

Table 4.4 Modification of the basic-salary progression in companies where the age limit is 60, by size of enterprise, 1985–7 (per cent of companies and years of age)

Patterns of modification	Average	1,000+	100–999	30–99
Modification implemented	52.6	84.9	57.9	48.5
Pattern A: Progression decreases	52.4	33.1	45.8	57.9
(Age)	(49.3)	(49.4)	(49.5)	(49.3)
Pattern B: Progression stops	23.0	17.3	23.4	23.3
(Age)	(52.1)	(54.3)	(52.4)	(51.7)
Pattern C: Salary decreases	8.9	8.5	12.3	6.9
(Age)	(53.0)	(53.2)	(52.6)	(53.4)
Pattern D: Salary lowered but progression from lower level	6.1	18.2	7.0	4.6
(Age)	(54.7)	(55.0)	(54.9)	(54.5)
Pattern E: Salary lowered and no progression anymore	4.8	8.0	5.2	4.2
(Age)	(54.1)	(55.4)	(54.5)	(53.6)
Others	3.9	14.5	6.0	1.8
(Age)	(45.6)	(47.1)	(46.0)	(44.1)

Note: Graphically, the different patterns show as follows:

Pattern A   B   C   D   E

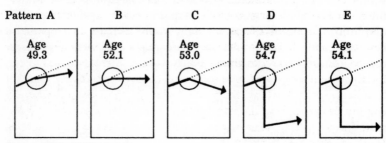

Source: MOL 1989i: 186–90

use. With the exception of overtime pay, monthly earnings remain largely independent of fluctuations in the business cycle. In addition, these earnings take into consideration the immediate social needs related to age and status. Most daily-life expenses are covered by monthly earnings. Deferred wage payments, though, are perceived differently. Expenses for durable goods and luxury items as well as savings are generally financed by the seasonal allowances. It is also common for large companies and associations of small enterprises to arrange some kind of housing loan with financial institutions to be available to regular employees, where the future separation allowance becomes the collateral and loan repayments are deducted from seasonal allowances. Thus the salary *system* itself plays a central role in influencing how the average Japanese envisions his and his family's quality of life.

The propensity of the Japanese people to save, as the high savings rates in postwar times have shown, can be largely attributed to the above-mentioned characteristics of the salary system. Gross saving rates for the period 1960–84 were 32.5 per cent in Japan, 23.7 per cent in West Germany, and 18.0 per cent in the United States (Balassa and Noland 1988: 83).

Various employee benefits are also provided. Some are statutory: health, pension, employment, and workmen's accident compensation insurances. Public benefits can be supplemented provided that certain conditions comply with the rules set by the labour union or employee association. These conditions concern the separation allowance and in many cases a private pension plan (combined with or in addition to the public pension system) as well as group life insurance. Such benefits are common in large firms; some small/medium firms provide them by pooling resources with other firms of similar size. Many firms also subsidize lunch, but the cost of commuting to work (via public transportation) is usually reimbursed. Benefits given voluntarily are considered to be a managerial prerogative but are often decided in conjunction with some employee organization. Thus dormitories for unmarried employees and company housing for families are made available at nominal rental rates. Furthermore, companies are known to provide or subsidize recreational activities for their employees and sponsor mutual-aid cooperatives. Another benefit offered that is fairly common is the system whereby employees can deposit their savings with the company to use as collateral for a housing loan or participate in a public programme on Workers' Property Accumulation.

Ninety per cent of all listed companies sponsor an Employee Stock Ownership Plan (ESOP) in which, on average, 40 per cent of the workforce participates. It is run by a permanent voluntary association of employees. The members decide on the amount they want to put towards stocks, which is usually deducted from their monthly pay, to which the company adds a premium. This amount is then used to purchase company shares at regular intervals (TSE 1990: 63). This ESOP is also quite common in small/medium enterprises, being 'more prevalent in the manufacturing industry (60.2 per cent) than in the service industry (36.4 per cent), in the unionized (58.5 per cent) than non-unionized sector (38.8 per cent)' (Osawa 1989: 7).

IN FOREIGN FIRMS

Foreign executives in Japan tend to view salaries in terms of a pay-as-you-go system rather than one which accepts the long-term liability. They perceive labour as a variable cost, not a fixed one. Moreover, they readily assume that they pay higher salaries than local competitors. A few years ago, the weekly English edition of what is respected as the Japanese equivalent of the *Wall Street Journal* reported that '[t]he per capita regular salary for June 1983 at foreign capitalized firms averaged ¥268,700, about ¥60,000 higher than that of Japanese firms' (*Japan Economic Journal*, 3 April, 1984). This information can be highly misleading to the home office of the foreign firm. For instance, *regular salary* is a term which can easily be misinterpreted. And, since years of service is a basic consideration in Japanese salaries, the average age of the company workforce must be known. But, due to greater mid-career recruiting, the average age in foreign firms is higher than that in Japanese counterparts. Furthermore, the age limit in some foreign companies is not in the standard 55–60 age range, but 65.

Wide discrepancies in compensation policies can be observed even among well-established foreign firms. As shown in a survey taken in 1985, '[o]ne firm pays no regular bonuses at all. Some pay bonuses at the same rate (in terms of percentage of annual salary) to employees of all grades. Others follow the Japanese practice of increasing the bonus rate with seniority. Some foreign affiliates pay higher family or housing allowance than the typical large Japanese firm; others do not pay these allowances at all' (IIBC 1987: 14). Other foreign companies blindly import home practices without considering the impact they will have, as can be seen in the case of incentives.

> Incentive payments – such as bonuses to sales personnel related directly to orders generated – is a common practice in the West and is often used by foreign affiliates in Japan. It is a rare practice among Japanese firms.... An analyst says: 'Generally, Japanese workers do not like incentive payments. Personnel managers of foreign affiliates often have difficulty in convincing top management that incentive payments do not necessarily give Japanese employees more incentive to work.' His point: the diligent will work anyway, and those who do not receive much incentive payments will be greatly discouraged. The foreign affiliates who continue to offer incentive payments apparently think otherwise. (*Ibid.*: 14–15)

In general, many an expatriate and those Japanese who do so to gain some immediate advantage, promote with missionary zeal the idea that monetary amounts (independent of the compensation *system*) are all that matter. As long as the workforce consists of only a few people, salaries can be decided on an individual basis. But this will not work with a larger workforce, when a managerial hierarchy becomes necessary. Without some overall *system*, salary amounts will be exposed to misunderstanding and will be attacked as a form of favouritism. Two situations in particular appear to have detrimental effects. First, as mentioned in Chapter 2, many of the employees are hired with work experience gained elsewhere and as bait are offered a salary decided outside the system. Second, supervisory promotion is too closely equated with salary increases; in terms of an overall balance, this causes indiscriminate increases in the basic salary, distorting the long-term implications. What is detrimental here is the practice of paying the monthly salary as a *flat* rate (without distinguishing monthly allowances), because this completely affects seasonal and separation allowances. Even more damaging to the company may be the Western practice of providing an *annual salary*, which is not recognized in Japan. In some extreme cases, when more concern is placed on international uniformity, the ways of the home office are put into practice in Japan. For example, the monthly salary is determined by the annual salary divided by 12, sometimes with a *bonus* at the end of the year. The higher monthly salary will be attractive, but the employee may leave within the first year because the company did not provide the standard seasonal allowances.

Contrary to their Japanese competitors, foreign firms often point out that overtime work by the non-supervisory staff is considered to be more of an exception, to the delight of the female employees. However, this could considerably reduce the take-home pay expected by middle-aged male employees. Also eliminated from the payroll is a flexibility that at times could be a convenience.

Finally, cash and non-cash benefits common to all large Japanese competitors (which labour unions and employees accept as standard, regardless of what the actual size of the foreign firm may be), are rarely given in the foreign firm. This disadvantage may, from the company's view, be lessened by higher salaries; however, from the employee's view, it may not.

At any rate, it could very well be an oversight to assume that the new graduates join foreign firms because of the higher starting salaries offered. For example, in April 1987, the average starting salary for a college graduate entering the foreign firm was ¥158,000 for males and ¥152,000 for females (MOL 1988b: 23 and 57); these amounts were two or three thousand yen higher than the averages offered by Japanese competitors. 'To a Japanese student who has yet to try his abilities, the traditional offer of a stable, predictable rise in earnings over the long term might seem the better choice' (IIBC 1987: 14). Overall, working conditions which include the prospect of stable employment are still more appealing.

Foreign firms may promote non-Japanese salary practices often out of an ignorance of the psychological and financial costs such practices incur on the company as well as out of a general lack of knowledge in established Japanese practices. Japanese managers in foreign firms may not raise objections, because if they do it could lead to their own financial demise.

APPENDIX I

EXAMPLE OF A TYPICAL BASIC SALARY TABLE

Customary every year, as a result of the Spring Wage Offensive (Chapter 6) and the recommendation by the National Personnel Authority (*Jinji-in*), the basic salary tables for civil servants are revised, i.e. all amounts are increased so that the average salary increase granted to government employees is reflected in the *total* revision. The table for government administrative staff, for example, was revised in September 1990 and made retroactive to April 1990 (Table 4.5).

Grades (represented by Roman numerals) and ranks (represented by Arabic numerals) are terms specific to salary administration; they relate to managerial hierarchy only indirectly. Whenever there is a change in an employee's salary, he is informed of it by a notice (*jirei*), which indicates his new grade and rank without any mention of a salary increase. It should be noted that government officials are one level higher in rank when compared alongside the private sector:

Government	Private sector
Shunin (experienced clerk)	*Kakari-chô* (sub-section chief)
Kakari-chô (sub-section chief)	*Ka-chô* (section chief)
Ka-chô (section chief)	*Bu-chô* (department head)
Shitsu-chô (chief of office)	(No exact equivalent)
Bu-chô (department head)	*Honbu-chô* (division head)

Grades (*shokumu no kyû*) are designated along the horizontal axis of

Table 4.5 Basic salary table of government administrative staff, FY 1990 (in yen)

Rank	I (Grade)	II	III	IV	V	VI	VII	VIII	IX	X	XI
1	–	–	157,300	185,100	201,500	220,300	238,400	258,200	289,600	325,500	371,000
2	113,600	143,100	163,400	193,200	210,200	229,300	247,600	267,900	301,400	338,200	386,500
3	117,300	149,900	169,800	201,400	219,100	238,300	256,900	277,700	313,200	350,900	402,000
4	121,200	157,200	176,400	210,000	227,700	247,400	266,300	287,600	325,000	363,700	417,400
5	125,600	162,900	183,200	218,800	236,300	256,500	275,800	297,700	337,000	376,600	432,800
6	130,800	167,700	190,700	227,300	244,800	265,600	285,300	307,800	349,000	389,500	448,200
7	136,100	172,500	198,100	235,600	253,300	274,800	294,900	317,900	361,200	402,500	463,600
8	141,200	177,300	205,400	243,800	261,600	284,100	304,600	327,900	373,400	415,300	479,000
9	145,300	181,500	211,800	251,700	270,000	293,400	314,300	337,900	385,400	428,000	493,900
10	148,600	185,800	217,900	259,500	278,200	302,900	323,900	347,900	397,100	440,000	508,800
(continues up to rank)	(16)	(19)	(30)	(28)	(26)	(24)	(22)	(21)	(18)	(15)	(15)

Note: In the original table, each grade lists subsequent amounts up to the rank indicated in ( ).
Source: NPA 1989b: 20

the table according to the nature of the work involved.

Grade   I   Clerical position assigned to routine duties
          II   Clerk with relatively high-level knowledge and experience
         III *Shunin* or clerk with very high-level knowledge and experience
         IV Sub-section chief or *Shunin* assigned to complex duties
          V Sub-section chief assigned to more complex duties
         VI Sub-section chief assigned to even more complex duties
        VII Deputy section chief
      VIII Deputy section chief assigned to complex duties
         IX Chief of office
          X Section chief or chief of office assigned to complex duties
         XI Department head or section chief assigned to very important tasks (NPA 1987: 4)

Higher positions, such as bureau chief and administrative vice minister, come under a different salary table.

Ranks (*gôhô*) are given along the vertical axis of the table and are essentially, but not exclusively, determined by years of service.

Starting salaries are determined according to the starting rates that prevail in the private sector and the results from entrance examinations taken for government employment. Grades and ranks are also determined according to these factors, as shown in Table 4.6.

Once starting salary is determined, it all becomes a matter of automatic progression. The basic salary increases every 12 months along the vertical axis (i.e. by rank). However, at certain points, a promotion

Table 4.6 The effects of entrance examinations on government starting salaries, grades and ranks

Examination	FY1986	FY1987	FY1988	FY1989	FY1990
Highest-level (taken by university graduates)	(II-2) 121,600	(II-2) 123,600	(III-1) 141,000	(III-1) 146,600	(III-1) 157,300
Middle level (usually taken by university graduates)	(II-1) 115,900	(II-1) 117,900	(II-1) 121,100	(II-1) 126,300	(II-2) 143,100
Lower level (usually taken by high school graduates)	(I-2) 97,800	(I-2) 97,500	(I-2) 102,200	(I-2) 106,600	(I-3) 117,300

in grade is expected. It is not normal for a given employee to remain in the same grade for more than the number of rankings provided in a given grade. For example, one would not be employed at the grade level I for more than 16 years.

An increase in rank is granted upon job performance evaluation, and an increase in grade is given according to added supervisory responsibilities. In the latter case, promotion in grade is given first, followed by the automatic increase in rank. For example, if the grade–rank of an employee was III–10 (¥217,900) in March 1991, then his salary increase in April would be decided in two steps. First, he would be promoted to a salary just above his in the next column, raising him to a level of IV–5 (¥218,800); next, the normal automatic increase would be given, boosting him to the level IV–6 (¥227,300).

In the case of government employees, average monthly earnings (in yen) were broken down in the manner shown in Table 4.7.

Table 4.7 Breakdown of average monthly earnings for government employees (in yen)

Components of monthly earnings	1986	1987	1988	1989	1990
Total	284,262	291,753	296,556	304,534	315,057
Basic salary (*honpô*)	246,977	253,330	257,382	264,364	272,657
Dependants' allowance (*fuyô teate*)	10,140	10,563	10,469	10,833	10,721
Adjustment allowance (*chôsei teate*)	12,443	12,925	13,194	13,561	14,152
Housing allowance (*jûkyo teate*)	1,661	1,705	1,923	2,159	2,304
Commutation allowance (*tsûkin teate*)	8,629	8,721	9,023	8,932	9,781
Others	4,412	4,509	4,565	4,685	5,442

Note: The adjustment allowance is paid to those assigned to areas where living costs are unusually high.
Source: NPA 1990 and previous years

5 Corporate organization

The employment system and the work environment shaped by it work together to create an effective style of corporate organization. According to organization development theory, there are two arche-types of organizational behaviour, mechanistic and organic (Kagono *et al.* 1985: 21–54). The mechanistic style of organization emphasizes bureaucratic dynamics, where great attention is paid to structure (division of labour and hierarchy of authority). Problems are solved by those at the top delegating responsibilities to those below, who continue the process of handing down duties that need to be performed. Characteristic of this style are the features related to the job itself (description, evaluation and compensation). Overlapping of tasks is discouraged; thus the tendency towards divisional structure (i.e. vertical control) is strong, and staffing is primarily specialist-oriented, where performance is closely tied to remuneration. Such an organizational style is superior in terms of efficiency: immediate results generated by the flow of authority.

The organic prototype of organizational style is where group dynamics play the leading role. Here, the process itself is the main concern, as problems are shared and solved on a step-by-step, trial-and-error basis. Upper management provides the general guidelines and incentives for participating in problem-solving. Not surprisingly, tasks overlap and preference is given to functional structure (horizontal coordination) and to generalists having interpersonal skills; performance is only vaguely linked to remuneration. The organic style of organization is considered superior to the mechanistic in terms of adaptability to environmental change, as emphasis is put on the flow of work and the process rather than on the flow of authority and the end results. The mechanistic style revolves around analysis and planning but the organic style centres on synthesis and experi-mentation (e.g. on-the-job training).

All organizations, including Japan's, have established themselves somewhere between these two prototypes. Close observation reveals that Western business organizations tend to exhibit the mechanistic style, and Japanese organizations the organic. As Table 5.1 shows, Western companies are preoccupied with financial considerations, i.e. mechanistic goals such as results, while Japanese companies prefer to emphasize market share, a more organic goal related to process. Japanese executives choose to stress not only the importance of market share but the means to obtain it, i.e. new product ratio. In fact, as their combined scores indicate, the importance they attach to these two goals (1.43 + 1.06 = 2.49) is comparable to the importance Americans and Europeans give to return on investment alone (2.43 and 2.51 respectively). The rapid development of the Japanese market has forced companies to rely less on the potential of products currently on the market and to direct their energies towards building their capacity for new product development. Moreover, management strategy has, since the mid-1970s, maintained an unwavering 70 per cent of its focus on the twin targets of increasing market share and promoting new product development, with emphasis significantly shifting from the former to the latter in recent years (MITI 1987b: 38).

When adapting to a more organic style of organization companies need a flexible structure which strengthens and promotes constant

Table 5.1 International comparison: importance of goals selected by management and ranking of top three

Management goals	US		Europe		Japan	
Return on investment*	2.43	①	2.51	①	1.24	②
Increase in share price*	1.14	②	0.70		0.02	
Increase in market share*	0.73	③	0.46		1.43	①
Improvement in product portfolio	0.50		0.85	②	0.68	
Efficient production and physical distribution*	0.46		0.81	③	0.71	
Debt/equity ratio	0.38		0.48		0.59	
New product ratio**	0.21		0.26		1.06	③
Corporate public image**	0.05		0.25		0.20	
Quality of working conditions***	0.04		0.40		0.09	

Note: Score average (top: 3 points; second: 2 points; third: 1 point; others: no points). Significant at level of t-test of means; *.05; **.01; ***.001. (Ranking of the top three goals was added.)
Source: Nonaka and Okumura 1984: 34

human interaction. Work is seen to be performed not in sequences but in a simultaneous manner. Throughout the system, *learning by doing* is the key. This allows the employee gradually to adapt and develop, with the assurance that he/she can depend on the experiences and commitment of subordinates, peers and even superiors at the cost of ignoring specific job descriptions. Control is exercised not so much by rules and procedures but by stressing that values and information need to be shared. Middle managers rather than upper management play the key role, not just as supervisors but more as coordinators. The evaluation of performance is measured on a collective scale which is based not on short-term results but on long-term potential, as the following example shows. Suppose a salesman's performance is evaluated at a score of 80. A new goal of 100 is set for the next sales period. At the end of this period his performance score rises to 90. There are two ways to look at his achievement: first, that 90 is ten points *below* the goal (a mechanistic approach, since the result is what matters); second, that 90 is ten points *above* the previous performance (an organic type of evaluation, where the process is more important; here, the new target is considered a success).

In the organic style of organization, the *development* of the human resource, i.e. the constant upgrading as its potential (rather than its mere management as a given resource) is the principal responsibility of the organization as a whole, including its labour union.

CORPORATE STRUCTURE

Organizational style is reflected in corporate structure. The Western corporate structure can be viewed in terms of a management-based structure divided into managerial ranks, where the hierarchy of upper, middle and lower management is determined by authority and responsibility. Management *is* the company. In Japanese corporations, corporate members (*sha-in*) also include the rank and file. The Japanese corporate structure is generally composed of three levels: a level of rank-and-file employees (*ippan sha-in*), who carry out operations, a level of managers (*kanri-sha*), who coordinate the operations, and a level of executives (*keiei-sha*), who work on strategic aspects. In diagrammatic form, the contrast is strikingly clear, as is shown in Figure 5.1.

Figure 5.1 Western and Japanese corporate structures compared

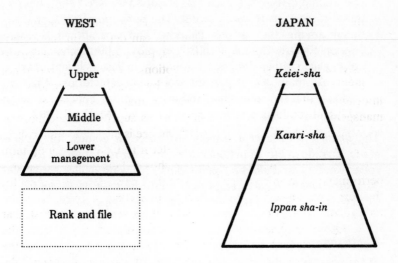

Ippan sha-in

Ippan sha-in are recognized as fully-fledged members of the corporate structure, since those at the upper levels had once started out their careers in much the same way some years back. The *ippan sha-in* contribute mainly to operational and logistic needs.

As noted in Chapter 3, the key requirement of employees at this level is that they receive extensive on-the-job training in order for them to be flexible in their skills and functions. This allows them to participate actively in managing their tasks (Chapter 7). Cohesion of the workgroup, which is reflected in the work itself, is the result they strive for.

Outstanding college-educated engineers are assigned in large numbers to the production line, and many are given an important say in business operations. Many manufacturing industry executives are engineers by training, and a majority have had extensive first-hand experience on the shop floor. As a result, they well understand the production line and the production process. Opinions and ideas coming up from the line are often reflected in development and design.... In addition, engineers involved in development and design always visit the production line, and talk things over with their counterparts on the floor. In Japan, even researchers are more likely to be found on the shop floor than in a research center; the majority of them are assigned to factories and operational divisions. Hitachi has about 8,000 R&D staff, but only 3,000 work at its research center. The remaining 5,000 are distributed among the various factories and operational divisions. Nippon Electric Company (NEC) employs 5,000 technicians who are engaged either directly or indirectly in research and development. As many as 90 percent work in the factories. What this means is that the connection and understanding between development and production is very smooth indeed. (Moritani 1982: 43)

The *ippan sha-in* level is usually structured in grades, for instance grade 1, grade 2, etc. Functional titles are *hanchô* (foreman) for blue-collar workers, and *shunin* (senior clerk) for white-collar employees. Non-supervisory regular employees perform their tasks under the supervision, or better yet, coordination of the *kanri-sha*.

Kanri-sha

This is the administrative level of management in charge of coordinating operations. The Japanese approach is illustrated by the open-room system commonly observed in Japanese offices, where managers sit together with their subordinates, a practice unthinkable to the Western firm. This kind of arrangement may also apply to executives, as in the case of the Honda Motor Company where, since 1964 at least, all top executives (in 1981, this included the president, three vice presidents, four senior managing directors, nine managing directors, and eleven directors for a total of twenty-eight executives; in January 1991, thirty-three executives) have worked in a large room about 300 sq. m, with no partitions, and when discussions took place tables were merely set up (Mito 1981: 27–8).

Traditionally, the main titles given at the *kanri-sha* level are: *kakari-chô* (sub-section chief), *ka-chô* (section chief) and *bu-chô* (department head). Several intermediate titles such as 'assistant' (*dairi* or *hosa*), 'deputy' (*fuku*), etc. are also given.

Such a hierarchical system has long been considered an important factor in supporting employee morale. In addition, in order to maintain this momentum, despite the surplus of candidates for these positions, many large companies have established, or simply adopted, a status hiearchy. The various levels are given titles such as, starting from the bottom, *shuji, shusa,* (these two appear to be interchangeable), *sanji,* and *riji.* None of these terms has an appropriate English translation; it can only be said that they simply indicate levels in a hierarchy where dynamism emerges from below rather than by autocratic influence from above.

About 10 per cent of the workforce in all industries are *kanri-sha*. The most important position at the *kanri-sha* level is that of *kachô* (section chief), whose practical purpose is to link policies with operations or, more specifically, executives with the rest of the company staff.

Keiei-sha

Top executives (*keiei-sha*) are corporate directors (*torishimari-yaku*) appointed to the Board of Directors (*torishimari-yakkai*), where they are given one of the following titles:

Torishimari-yaku	Director
Jômu	Managing Director
Semmu	Executive Managing Director
Fuku sha-chô	Executive Vice President (usually just one)
Sha-chô	President, also Representative Director
Kai-chô	Chairman of the Board

By law, the Board must include one or more statutory auditors (*kansa-yaku*). The inclusion of outside directors on the Board is not that common a practice; 40 per cent of large manufacturing companies and 60 per cent of large retailers have no outside directors (MITI 1987b: 32 and MITI 1987c: 28). If outside directors are present they have most likely been sent by financial institutions and trading companies and, more often than not, their purpose is to reinforce the interlocking of corporate directorates, which is commonly done within industrial groups.

> For example, as of March 1982, the top six trading companies had dispatched executives to 57.3 per cent of the companies in which they held 10 per cent or more of the shares (an average of 1.4 directors per company or 14.2 per cent of the Board), to 89.6 per cent of their affiliates (2.7 directors per company or 30.1 per cent of the Board), and to 97.6 per cent of their subsidiaries (5 directors per company or 66.2 per cent of the Board) (FTC 1983: 32)

Aoki described the strategic role of the *keiei-sha* in the following terms:

[The] mediating role [of executives] ... extends beyond the internal organization and they [the executives] must engage in a mediating function of higher order, between the qualitatively different constituent bodies of the [Japanese] firm, the stockholders of diverse background, the body of quasi-permanent employees, suppliers and dealers in relational contracting, and others. They are expected to deliver a reasonable rate of return to stockholders ... dealers, and suppliers ... as well as reasonable earnings and promotabilities to quasi-permanent employees ... and research opportunities for researchers and engineers.... At this stage, not only their arbitrative skill, but also entrepreneurial leadership will count as an increasingly important qualification for the top job, since the economic success of the firm, gauged by the market performance of the product, is the ultimate requisite for satisfying the economic needs of the diverse constituent bodies of the firm. (Aoki 1988: 255)

In larger companies, the ultimate decision-making power resides with the Executive Committee (*jômu-kai*), which is composed of managing directors and those in higher ranks, a practice imported from the United States after World War II; in other companies this privilege resides with the Board itself.

Except for the rare instance when the chairman also holds the title of representative director (*daihyô torishimari-yaku*), the chief executive officer (CEO) is the president. In the 1980s, in large manufacturing companies, his average age was slightly over 60; however, his term as president was seven to nine years (MITI 1987b: 29). He normally appoints his successor at the time he retires.

Great attention is paid to the *origins* of company presidents by Japan's business world. Basically, in the case of manufacturing, their origins fall into the following categories (figures in parentheses refer to the rate of occurence):

1 Founders of the company (13.6 per cent in 1974 and 4.6 per cent in 1986);
2 'Second generation,' i.e. the son, son-in-law, or grandson of the founder (17.4 per cent in 1974 and 24.2 per cent in 1986);
3 'True-born,' i.e. those who joined the company upon graduation (28.4 per cent in 1974 and 40.6 per cent in 1986);
4 Transferred from another company (40.6 per cent in 1974 and 30.6 per cent in 1986); reportedly, the lowest performers (MITI 1987b: 28).

The influence of shareholders' meetings on the selection and supervision of management is quite limited.

> The shareholder in the [Japanese corporation] is in the position of an investor, but in no operational sense in control of the company .... [The company] becomes in a real sense the property of the people who make it up. It will not be sold, in whole or in part, without the specific approval of all of its directors, acting on behalf of its employees. Earnings of the company go first as a return to investors, with the entire balance going to ensure the company's future and thus ensure the future of its employees. (Abegglen and Stalk 1985: 191, 207–8)

CORPORATE HEADQUARTERS

In the organic style of corporate organization, the Head Office (*honsha*) plays a more central role than where the style of organization is mechanistic. In large corporations it has its own staff of well over one thousand, if not two thousand.

The *hon-sha* is organized in the following way:

1 Top management directly supported by the planning and control staff;
2 General Affairs Department (*Sômu-bu*) in charge of office management, custodial services, shareholder affairs, public relations, and government affairs; often, it is also given charge of legal affairs, international affairs, personnel, and sometimes finance;
3 Special departments: personnel, finance and marketing; and
4 Service staff (computing services, etc.).

Overall, the staffing of indirect departments is substantial. This should not be interpreted merely as the centralization of control and authority. The Japanese attitude towards authority has distinct characteristics, which lies behind the fact that the Japanese word for authority has two different terms, *ken-i* and *kengen*. As noted by a sociologist, the former stands for

> [T]he influence arising from circumstances, in particular the character, status prestige, or title of the person.... [The latter stands for] the right, validated by certain rules or consensus, to issue orders, and which is to be exercised within a defined, limited scope.... [It] can be interpreted as a set of rights and power granted to a person to carry out a delegated job and which must be

respected, within the defined scope, by both his superiors and subordinates. (Iwata 1982: 3–4)

Whereas *kengen* may be sufficient in obtaining the acceptance of orders, *ken-i* is preferred by the organic style of Japanese organization, for not only is it effective it also suits the 'exceptionally strong presence of "solidarity of responsibility" among the members of a family, university, private firm and other types of groups' (*Ibid.*: 2). This outlook is reflected in the following episode typical of Japanese corporate behaviour.

> In mid-1984, the New York branch of a large Japanese bank incurred a loss in foreign exchange transactions of $40 million, roughly equivalent to the monthly profit of the bank. Responsibility was assumed as follows: (1) profit-sharing for all 34 members of the board of directors in Tokyo including the chief executive officer was canceled, though most of them were not even involved in international business; (2) the senior managing director and managing director of the international office, who were based in Tokyo, were demoted to managing director and to director respectively; (3) the general manager of the New York branch was fired because he had full responsibility for the branch; (4) the branch officer (manager) was transferred back to Tokyo; and (5) the assistant manager who handled the transactions directly was fired. (Watanabe and Mochizuki 1986: 88)

Scholars have pointed out that when Japan imported the Western legal system in the last century the word for rights, a notion fundamental to Western law, did not exist in the Japanese language. Transliterated as *ken-ri*, this is the term used today (Tanaka 1976: 305). For centuries, relations among the Japanese people had been asserted not on rights but on duties.

LEARNING ENVIRONMENT

Lifetime employment is just one manifestation of the organic organization. It not only supports the overall concern for a constant upgrading of the workforce but makes such a view a prerequisite in nurturing the talents necessary to manage innovation and to respond to changes in the environment. In the absence of a contractual *quid pro quo* (i.e. remuneration measured by performance), to employ someone does not mean to look for a person fitting a given job description but rather to see what kind of work would be best suited to the employee.

The company therefore has the responsibility to provide continuous training and upgrading. The main task is to encourage collective learning, and the easiest way this is done is through the sharing of knowledge acquired from a wide range of work experience and from job rotation. And so it follows that *learning by doing* is how the child began to write, how the nation started to industrialize, and how the corporate member today gains his skills.

On-the-job training

Expectations run high in on-the-job training (OJT). Problems are discussed and solved by trial and error. Duties overlap and tend to be carried out simultaneously, and gradually adaptive behaviour begins to develop that can rely on the experience and commitment of fellow-workers. In order to accomplish this, preference must then be given to functional structure (horizontal coordination) and to generalists. Performance appraisal focuses not on the short-term performance of a *specialist* but on the long-term potential of a *generalist*, as exemplified by the open-room system referred to earlier.

> In fact, the [Japanese] firm has increasingly delegated work control to the shopfloor level since the mid-1960s and has encouraged workers to solve problems by themselves whenever possible. Individual workers are authorized to stop a production line when necessary. The number of specialists – such as repairmen, product inspectors, and technicians – has been reduced as much as possible, and, when necessary, their expertise is used to help shopfloor workers solve a particular problem; thus they act as consultants rather than performing a special function exclusively. (Aoki 1988: 16)

For college graduates, a long-term job rotation means an 18-month to two-year posting. The Personnel Department first chooses these posts and later defines them under the supervision of senior managers so as to make an optimal selection in the long run. From start to finish, much of the teaching is done by the senior lecturing the junior; such teaching is considered a requisite for further promotion.

> When a new product is being produced, or a production system rearranged, a taken-for-granted part of the production engineering involved is for engineers and work study experts to hold formal sessions to explain the changes, and to instruct – as hands-on as is necessary – those who have to do something new just how that new

thing is to be done.... [A] good deal of cross-departmental lecturing [is involved] – designers explaining the principles of their designs to assemblers; testers exlaining the testing criteria to the electricians who have to design the equipment, etc. (Dore and Sako 1989: 90–1)

Off-the-job training

In addition, off-the-job training is provided for white-collar and for selected blue-collar workers in order to systematize the insights gained through experience. Most large firms have established elaborate training centres for their regular employees. The corporate policy at one major electronics manufacturer maintains that any engineer's knowledge is obsolete every three years and thus requires re-training. The following example, obtained through an interview, is not unusual. In the aerospace industry, a major American company wanted to cultivate strategic contacts with its counterpart in Japan. Their expatriate representative asked the Japanese company to propose names of engineers who for a period of one or two years would work together with their American counterparts. The Japanese side submitted the names along with the research papers they had written for internal examination. These reports were translated into English, and the American side accepted them as doctoral level. They thus proceeded with obtaining visas. But working permits were refused on the account that the candidates had only a high school degree; that their status of *engineer* had been earned through internal training was irrelevant.

Correspondence courses are very popular, and the revision of the Vocational Training Law (1984) allows some 1,200 courses to qualify for subsidization by the Ministry of Labour. A large majority of them develop administrative and technical skills and are run by private institutions.

Small firms have access to public and semi-public vocational training programmes, most of them sponsored by local governments that provide assistance by offering the use of public facilities, sending instructors, and subsidizing operational costs, including the cost of training materials. Subsidies are also given directly to small enterprises who send their employees to these programmes (Umetani 1980: 40).

The organic nature of Japanese business organization cannot, however, be limited to a phenomenon only internal to the organization. No living organism can survive outside the appropriate environment.

Top executives are ready to shoulder the blame for mistakes made by subordinates not as the result of some enlightened altruism; the company expects them to, just as the society expects them to. In Western industrial societies selected individuals are fully dedicated to business pursuits; in Japan this tendency is widespread and strongly supported by a collective effort. And this is true at all levels. Upon retirement, high government officials are seen as 'coming down from the heavens' (*ama-kudari*) to contribute their expertise to business enterprises. Top executives participate actively in the major national and regional business organizations as well as in the numerous deliberation boards (*shingikai*) sponsored by government agencies. Managers also act as officers in trade and industry associations. Even some factory and office workers are personally involved in the local chapters of the quality-control movement (Cole 1989: 282–95). These are all expensive propositions, but companies gladly absorb the costs because what is brought back into the work environment is not only a personally satisfied individual seeking to be an active partici- pant in the industrial society, but also the corporate image that the company is indeed part and parcel of the same industrial society.

RETAINING REGULAR EMPLOYEES

Japanese companies regard *regular* employees as their fundamental asset and, as a consequence, endeavour constantly to upgrade it. Their concern is to retain these employees and keep them loyal to the company. Enterprise unions and their substitute, the employee associations, contribute substantially to maintaining stability in the regular workforce. 'In the manufacturing sector, the separation rate in the unionized sector is 4.6 per cent lower than that in the non-union- ized sector, while the difference in the service sector is 4.8 per cent' (Osawa 1989: 6). In the Japanese fashion so well established, corporate loyalty is more a collective imperative than an individual virtue.

> [A] concern with reputation plays an important role in helping both the employer and employee cope with ... restraining the premature quitting of trained employees.... [B]ecause of adverse selection, employees who quit spoil their reputation and incur a high separation cost. Outsiders who reemploy them also treat them as low-productivity, low-motivation types. I submit, however, that Japanese firms, particularly large and established ones, have bound themselves to an implicit code of not hiring former employees of

other firms, particularly skilled ones, so that ranking hierarchy at each firm can function effectively as an incentive to discourage skilled employees from quitting. (Aoki 1988: 82–3)

Internal communication is of the utmost importance and explicitly cultivated in order to enhance the attractiveness of the workplace. It starts immediately at the time of hiring. In large companies, every April brings in dozens if not hundreds of high-school and college graduates who enter to spend several months together in in-house training programmes, where they develop a strong *esprit de corps.* This feeling will be reinforced in the years ahead by living in company dormitories where *skinship* is fostered among technicians, clerks, engineers and operators who eat, sleep and relax together. Later, the camaraderie 'takes the form of small gatherings of colleagues who entered the company in the same year and may be scattered throughout a number of company operations: production, marketing, research, general affairs. Getting together at a bar after hours, they often have informal discussions about their work before turning to songs and less serious talk' (Moritani 1982: 45). Alumni of the same school, technicians and sales representatives, the section chief and his subordinates, etc., also spend their after-hours together. Comradeship is fostered between male employees through social activities, often at the cost of family life. But it is in this after-hour context that the relationship between *sempai* and *kôhai* (senior–junior) flourishes, furthering a deep sense of security between the two, where the senior provides assistance to the junior who, in turn, supports him. This can often result in the formation of a clique (*habatsu*), only to become immersed in competition with other cliques (Chapter 6). However, one thing is certain: work-related communication is effectively exchanged between people in spite of their different specialities and different organizational units.

[F]or a Japanese, his main circle of friends and colleagues comes from the same company and his life outside the organization he belongs to is extremely limited. Thus, one's working life represents a large portion of one's whole life. So, for many Japanese, it is a joy to work together with his colleagues and an even greater joy to be highly regarded by them. In this way, the concept of work is very different from that of the Westerners. In other words, for the Japanese work and play are not completely separated from one another. Therefore, rather than a style of working only during the prescribed working hours and using the rest of the time for one's private life, most Japanese prefer working like the dickens when things are busy and then taking it easy when things are dull. Nor do they mind thinking about work outside of office or factory hours. (Iwata 1982: 81)

A formal means of communication is the workshop meeting, where superior and subordinate can interact (which happens to be a practice that many Japanese companies are trying to introduce in their overseas establishments). For example, at the start of the workday, the section; division or plant gathers for brief pep-talks by fellow-workers and a quick review of the previous day's events, as well as to go over the schedule for the day.

Many companies have also adopted the practice of giving out awards, such as the company president's award (*shachô-shô*), branch head's award (*shitenchô-shô*), or other ones recognizing particular sub-units of the organization. 'These are often given to entire units within the organization and are usually given weekly, monthly or annually, often as a reward for outstanding performance during a particular accounting period' (Mouer and Sugimoto 1989: 171).

IN FOREIGN FIRMS

Organizational style is a problem for foreign firms because it clearly affects the entire staff of the business entity. The problem is often presented directly to either the home office or the expatriate excutives in Japan, when in fact it concerns local employees as well (unless, of course, the multinational corporation decides to play all its cards according to its own view of international strategy).

A preoccupation with direct results, a short-term approach, is often at the heart of the problem. A tough lesson taught by Japanese competitors in relation to strategy is that process, i.e. a long-term approach, is more important than results. For example, a comparison of key success factors in the principal lines of business showed that American executives ranked product (result-oriented) strategy at the top, whereas Japanese executives also gave product strategy the same score but ranked production (process-oriented) strategy as number one (Table 5.2).

The foreign firm tends to stress control in the form of authority (*kengen*), maintaining it not only under the presence of expatriates but also with rules and procedures. Communication with the home office thus requires an extensive use of figures. Plans varying in length cover each corporate function which is handled by the budget and supported by periodic reports that keep track of these operations – a

Table 5.2 International comparison: key success factors in the principal business and their ranking

Key success factors	US Mean and rank		Japan Mean and rank	
Product strategy (product planning; market research for new products; R&D, etc.)	3.65	①	3.66	②
Production strategy (economies of scale; cost reduction; flexibility of production system, etc.)	3.46	②	3.80	①
Pricing strategy (price policy, pricing decision, etc.)	3.27	③	2.98	③
Promotion strategy (sales management and personal selling; advertising and other marketing communications strategies)	2.79	④	2.77	④
Distribution strategy (choice of distribution channel; distribution and inventory programme, etc.)	2.71	⑤	1.78	⑤

Note: Scores: 5 (the most important) to 1 (the least important) strategic factor.
Ranking added.
Source: Kagono *et al*. 1985: 34

very mechanistic approach. The problem is manifold: Who prepares the plans? Who administers the budget? Who writes the reports? And when the corporate controller comes to Japan to check the books he must, first, talk with the chief accountant (a position which rarely exists in Japanese companies) and, second, review the books. Both activities, of course, take place in English ... almost taking for granted that local managers, tax administrators, etc. can adjust their way of thinking and their behaviour from a Japanese to an English mode whenever they are called upon by a non-Japanese.

The Japanese are perplexed by the mechanistic approach of Western companies, where investment and operations are controlled by a division rather than by the corporation itself. In fact, they are amazed to learn that representatives from two divisions of a given foreign company doing business with the same local company visit Japan at the same time unbeknown to each other. The final result is that the corporate structure of the home office is reinstituted in Japan without much ado.

As mentioned in Chapter 4, foreign firms generally tend to consider the *buchô* level as the most important level in operations management (and thus their pay becomes disproportionate to others, jeopardizing the salary *system*), whereas their Japanese competitors stress the same importance in regards to the *kachô* level. Mid-career hiring from a Japanese company tends to become easier in the later age brackets (40 and over), when the potential candidate realizes that the *buchô* position is out of the question in the Japanese company where he is employed but that the position is now offered to him as bait by a foreign firm. By accepting, the new manager may experience a temporary satisfaction but his new subordinates will feel frustrated in their own ambitions. The mid-career hiring may set off a ripple effect that extends all the way down to the new graduates who have just joined. Such a situation may be resented by all regular employees as a clear denial of the organic nature of the organization.

Localization of management is not the answer if it means simply replacing expatriates with Japanese; concern should be placed on shifting to a more organic style of organization, which will be discussed in a later chapter as establishing a local corporate presence that transcends the obvious aspects of operations (Chapter 10).

6 Career in management

In the early postwar years, the differences with prewar business practice were clearly noticeable and much was written about Japanese management evolving into a profession. Today, however, there is still scepticism in calling it a profession. Given the existing corporate culture, managers and executives are expected to start at the bottom of the corporate structure to acquire gradually the managerial capacity necessary for corporate effectiveness. Experience is stressed over knowledge, for in an organic organization, management is not considered a profession, but is instead perceived in relation to status.

The development of managerial status is primarily a corporate responsibility, not only out of necessity but also for the well-being of the company. As a rule, promotion is based on a system of moving up the ranks, while executives are developed under job rotation and off-the-job training. In this way, not only is technical diversification emphasized, the company's experience in operations and personnel is broadened as well. Managers are regularly asked to present lectures regarding their duties to new as well as seasoned employees in a formal training session for all, teachers and pupils alike. At the same time, management development is provided both inside and outside the company.

Companies and their executives belong to industrial and trade associations, management development organizations, and prestigious organizations such as the Federation of Business Organizations (*Keidanren*) and the Japan Association of Corporate Executives (*Keizai Dôyûkai*). These organizations provide the opportunity for executives to meet their counterparts from other firms, and this creates a foundation for mutual cooperation and understanding and may help them in achieving mutual satisfaction. When and if it seems that an individual manager is being considered for the post of director (normally in his fifties), he must still be able to show that he is capable of dealing successfully with the business environment. Thus, he will have to keep abreast of the constant changes in a dynamic society and economy while participating in a multitude of activities offered by Japan's business world. Depending on his ability, he may be selected for an executive position in some industrial association. If he demonstrates skill at arbitrating the interests of member firms, he may then be asked to take an executive position at *Keidanren* and participate in various official deliberation boards. By this time, he will generally have retired from active duty with his company, although he may still continue to perform duties under the title of advisor. With pride, he will devote all his energy towards fulfilling his role as mediator.

PERFORMANCE AND PROMOTION

Advancement in the long and loyal careers of most Japanese managers is fundamentally controlled by length of service. The average age among them is rising steadily; currently it is 50 for the *buchô* and 46 for the *kachô* (Table 6.1). There is no short cut available even for the more capable, but in later years a difference in the rate of promotion emerges depending on ability, although the difference is not very great.

Until the first oil crisis (1973), promotion was open to all college graduates, at least until the level of *kachô*. Those less successful might reach this position in their late forties, remaining there until retirement; others might be promoted to a side line under the title of *specialist*. Companies adhering to more traditional ways maintain a

Table 6.1 Average age of buchô and kachô by size of enterprise, 1980–90

Year	500 or more employees (A)		Less than 500 employees (B)		Average of (A) and (B)	
	Buchô	Kachô	Buchô	Kachô	Buchô	Kachô
1980	49.0	43.0	48.3	42.4	48.9	42.9
1984	50.0	43.9	48.5	43.3	49.8	43.8
1986	50.3	44.1	48.3	43.4	50.0	43.9
1988	50.5	44.5	48.8	43.2	50.3	44.3
1989	51.0	46.0	49.1	45.5	50.5	45.9
1990	50.6	45.8	49.7	44.7	50.4	45.5

Source: NPA 1990 and previous years

Figure 6.1 Promotion pattern at an insurance company: 27 male university graduates hired in 1955

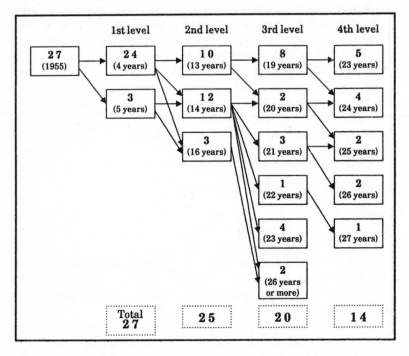

Note: The total declines over the years as some employees fail to be promoted and others leave.
Source: Adapted from *Nikkei Business* 1989: 90

pattern, even today, whereby promotion is consistently delayed. For example, the most qualified candidates reach the fourth level of promotion after more than 20 years in the company; those less qualified will take an additional five years, if they have not already lost momentum at a lower level or left the company altogether (Figure 6.1). On the other hand, the more progressive corporations have already been experimenting with a pattern of promotion that allows the underdog candidate to be brought back into more favourable bounds (Figure 6.2).

After 1973, however, the economic growth rate slowed down, forcing corporations into 'trimming the fat' (*genryô keiei*), which largely eliminated automatic promotion. In the 1980s, companies registered their concern over the loss of motivation apparently resulting from the delay in management promotions owing to the lack

Figure 6.2 Promotion pattern at Honda Motor: 48 male university graduates hired in 1960

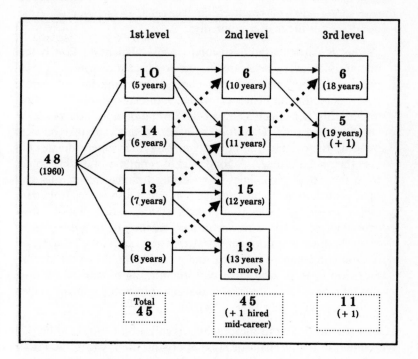

Note: The total declines over the years as some employees fail to be promoted and others leave. (+1) means a mid-career hired employee.
Source: Adapted from *Nikkei Business* 1989: 89

of openings at each promotional level. What further complicates the problem is that the baby-boom generation is now in its late thirties and eligible for promotion, which means that there are too many candidates and not enough positions. Today each promotional step tends to require written tests and interviews. In many large firms all managers come up for review at about the age of 45. Those who are less successful may be offered incentives for early retirement.

More significant than standard promotional criteria is the impact of the superior/subordinate relationship. The organic nature of the Japanese corporate organization discounts the simple expedient of delegating authority from above, since experience (i.e. years of service) is what promotes long-term relationships, thereby giving it greater importance. The superior becomes bound to his subordinates not so much by the flow of authority but rather by the flow of work that creates a network of mutual obligations. The superior knows that he gained his position through the support given to him by his subordinates more than as a result of his own capacity or potential. Aoki, again, describes the matter pointedly:

> [W]hat is particularly conspicuous in the [Japanese] firm is that managers at every level are subject to strict monitoring by both peers and subordinates. If a manager of any rank fails to build a good reputation and elicit emotional support from his/her subordinates, his/her effectiveness in the formal organization would be curtailed over time. Therefore, managers at any rank take pains to build up their reputation not only among their superordinates but also their subordinates. A good part of reputation building comes from their own capabilities in specialized management roles and their contributions to the organization, but it also comes from their ability to delegate decision-making to the satisfaction of their subordinates and to strike a proper balance of interests among them. In other words, one may say that an important consideration in evaluating managers in the promotional hierarchy of the [Japanese] firm is their arbitrative performance, as monitored by their subordinates. The successful managers are normally highly skilled in this respect. (Aoki 1988: 254)

Leadership according to the organic organization is not like the pull type found in the mechanistic style of organization, where the leader sets the goal and then pulls the group by standing above his subordinates to *supervise*. In the organic organization the leader places himself inside the group and pushes it toward the common goal, not so much in a supervisory role as by *coordinating* the initiatives collected from below. This superior/subordinate relation also instills more deeply the common objective of corporate survival (see Figure 6.3).

In Japanese companies, promotion to managerial levels is considered with the following in mind:

1 Something all candidates have in common is a relatively high level of education, but after about a decade of service in the company the rate of promotion proceeds at different rates according to individual evaluation.
2 Promotion is a step-by-step process, where the long-term potential of the candidate is the basic concern. Promotion is seen to reflect a stage of development rather than as a position gained.
3 Competence is directly related to experience (rather than knowledge) in handling available resources, especially the human

Figure 6.3 Pull and push leadership

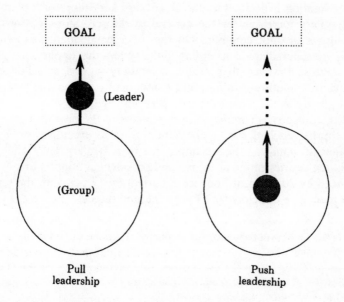

resource. This requires a competency level that can be applicable to the many functions of the company.

4 Finally, promotion is not determined solely by a particular individual's performance, since each candidate is without question evaluated against his peers.

Personal interaction is thus the ultimate test of managerial performance. The simplest way to measure it is to monitor the manager's skill in handling the decision-making process. The main thing to watch for is to see how he encourages active participation amongst all those concerned, not just in formulating a decision but in following through to the end the course of action deemed necessary by all. In fact, a successful manager is skilled at stimulating and regulating the flow of information, traits which are more important to collective performance rather than decision-making (Chapter 7).

'Money is not an important motivation. What is important for motivating Japanese top management is the job itself, and the social prestige of the position, both of which are derived by the success of the corporation. As measurements of success, the growth rate, the size of the firm and profit rates on sales are considered important, and top managers work hard for this purpose' (Kono 1984: 36). This kind of motivation is common among all regular employees, and salary differentials are not the major incentives. Executive (*keiei-sha*) compensation is decided by the Board and kept more or less in line with salary increases for the general workforce. Stock options for executives are not common. On the other hand, managers (*kanri-sha*) are generally paid according to the system that applies to regular employees; however, they receive a monthly supervisory allowance. Individual monthly earnings, and consequently seasonal allowances, vary greatly by the size of the enterprise and age.

If a company is compelled to make cuts in the payroll it starts at the top by reducing the compensation given to executives, followed by that of managers. For example, between January 1983 and July 1984 the salaries of the chairman and president at Nippon Steel were reduced by 20 per cent, the vice president by 17 per cent, the senior and managing directors by 13 per cent, and directors by 11 per cent.

Table 6.2 Outline of two university graduates' successful careers in manufacturing

Case I Age	Period	(Degree in mechanical engineering) Assignment
23–4	10 days	Orientation
	18 months	In charge of assembling parts needed in the operation of a major piece of equipment
24–6	3 years	Developing operations for the same equipment but for different parts
27–8	2 years	Inspecting final stage of machine assemblies; offered suggestions that reduced defects by 30 per cent
29–32	4 years	Supervise operation of three machines for processing parts
33–5	3 years	Posted to one of the sales offices as a member of technical support staff
36–7	2 years	Promoted to *kakari-chô* in the same sales office
38–42	5 years	Transferred to head office, Sales Department; promoted to *kakari-chô*
43–9	7 years	Reassigned to plant where he first started; promoted to *ka-chô* in charge of manufacturing
50–5	6 years	Promoted to plant manager
56–8	3 years	Receives additional title: *torishimari-yaku*
59 ...		Retirement; takes position as president at a major subsidiary

Case II	(Degree in accounting)	
Age	Period	Assignment
22–3	10 days	Orientation
	2 years	Posted to Sales Office in Osaka
24–6	3 years	Transferred to a plant in Tokyo; procuring materials (level of English proficiency recognized)
27–8	18 months	Transferred to head office, International Department; export section
28–31	3 years	Sent to UK subsidiary, Accounting Department, as *kakari-chô*
32–7	6 years	Return to head office, Accounting Section; promoted to *kachô*, responsible for consolidated statements
38–42	5 years	Transferred to Finance Department (head office); promoted to *buchô dairi*
43–50	8 years	Transferred to Planning Department (head office); promoted to *buchô*
51–3	3 years	Transferred to General Affairs Department (head office) as *buchô*
54–7	4 years	Receives additional title: *torishimari-yaku*
58 ...		Retirement at the mandatory age of 58; takes position as *semmu*

Until June 1984 salaries of all managers had been reduced by 10 per cent. Other steel companies enforced similar reductions. For the *ippan sha-in* there was no compensation for overtime work (*Asahi Shimbun*, July 1984). Amidst the difficulties adjusting to the rapid appreciation of the yen (1985–6), the salaries of executives and managers were reduced in one out of five large manufacturing companies (MITI 1987b: 83).

A MANAGERIAL CAREER

The manager generally is male – in fact, less than 10 per cent of managerial personnel are female. In tracing the successful managerial career in a large company, a common pattern emerges.

In his twenties the new employee formally enters the company on 1 April, welcomed under an elaborate rite of passage lasting for several days. At this point, he is recognized as a *shakai-jin*, or fully-fledged, responsible adult member of society. For at least several months his initial training will be at the most basic level of operations. This means that in a manufacturing company he may be placed on the production line, and in a bank he may be given the duty of collecting deposits door to door. Every two or three years he can expect to be moved between departments and sections under titles such as senior clerk or first-line supervisor (*shunin*).

In his mid-thirties he is promoted to *kakari-chô* (sub-section chief), and a few years later to *ka-chô* (section chief). Promotions at this time serve to recognize the responsibility for coordinating different tasks.

In his late-forties he is promoted to *bu-chô* (department head) at least twice, first in one and then in another department, the second being of greater importance.

In his mid-fifties he receives the title of *torishimari-yaku* (director), indicating that in addition to his operational responsibilities he is recognized as a member of top management. Like all other regular employees, he receives his separation allowance when giving up his position as *bu-chô* at the mandatory age limit. He now participates as a full-time member of the Board of Directors. Two university graduates' successful careers in manufacturing of university graduates are outlined in Table 6.2.

IN FOREIGN FIRMS

Most foreign firms have both expatriate as well as Japanese executives and managers. Expatriates are preferred by these companies for two reasons: the need for clear communication (language and business contacts, transfer of knowhow, etc.) with the home office and the lack of international expertise on the part of the Japanese. A practical transition would be to take a team approach combining a Japanese executive who is in charge of the downstream side, i.e. all local operations, with an expatriate who for two or three years is responsible for upstream relations with the home office.

Foreign managers

In 1988, expatriates numbered 522 out of 2,631 executives (19.8 per cent) and 493 out of 22,331 managers (2.2 per cent) (Table 6.3). In

Table 6.3 Foreign firms: number of directors and employees, and ratio of foreigners, 1987 and 1988

Industry and year		No. of firms	Directors		Employees			
			Number	Foreign (ratio)	Number	Foreign (ratio)	Number	Foreign (ratio)
All	1987	1,052	2,631	522 (19.8)	132,985	1,015 (0.7)	22,331	493 (2.2)
	1988	1,282	3,151	582 (18.5)	169,024	1,337 (0.8)	30,328	885 (2.9)
Manufacture	1987	507	1,481	256 (17.3)	103,753	521 (0.5)	16,048	254 (1.6)
	1988	618	1,781	277 (15.6)	132,190	684 (0.5)	22,206	464 (2.1)
Commerce	1987	396	841	202 (24.0)	21,913	357 (1.6)	4,963	132 (2.7)
	1988	519	1,073	258 (24.0)	28,796	587 (2.0)	6,776	372 (5.5)
Services	1987	116	236	47 (19.9)	5,309	105 (2.0)	1,153	17 (1.5)
	1988	112	225	34 (15.1)	6,845	58 (0.8)	1,086	43 (4.0)
Others	1987	33	73	17 (23.3)	2,010	32 (1.6)	931	89 (9.6)
	1988	33	72	13 (18.1)	1,193	8 (0.7)	260	6 (2.3)

Source: MITI 1989a: 166–7; and 1990c: 140–1

general, their number increases as the size of the company gets smaller, and the higher the foreign capital ratio the higher the proportion of expatriate presidents. Among foreign firms, those of American origin employed more expatriates than their non-American counterparts. In 1987, the percentage of foreigners among general employees was 4.0 per cent, in management positions 5.2 per cent, among full-time executives 19.9 per cent, and acting as presidents or branch managers 33.4 per cent (MOL 1989a: 12 and 62).

The main shortcoming of employing the expatriate is, not surprisingly, the relatively short duration of his stay in Japan. In American companies his contract is usually for two or three years, whereas in European companies it is commonly twice as long. Family problems of the expatriate can also create difficulties. At the same time, home offices all too often envision unrealistic ambitions. Strategic solutions (for example with regard to global production and/or marketing) are expected from the man out on the field, as he is expected to be well-versed in the tactics of fierce competition characterizing the Japanese market. Moreover, it is estimated that at least 70 per cent of the time and energy of the resident foreign executive is absorbed by communication with the home office and responsibilities in hosting overseas guests.

The management set-up of the foreign firm may be inhibiting effective operations. Whether the company is a joint venture or a wholly owned subsidiary, a Board of Directors is legally required. Too frequently, however, it only amounts to a formality. Even the annual meeting that is legally required is assembled *pro forma*, since many of the foreign directors do not reside in Japan. In a joint venture, this meeting is actually a shareholders' meeting between the parent companies. Thus management decisions are obviously not taken in the local context. As a result, the corporate image is definitely weak in the eyes of the local staff as well as other local contacts.

Japanese managers

As mentioned in previous chapters, extensive mid-career hiring is a drawback. In reputable Japanese firms the rule that persists is (with the number of exceptions slowly on the rise) that promotion occurs from within the ranks; the hiring of managers is considered an exception to the rule (Chapter 2). Foreign firms, however, out of necessity, make the exception the rule. But its direct consequence in relation to the salary system is visible in the growing imbalance between the pay of section chiefs (*kachô*) and department heads (*buchô*) which erodes the *unity* of the workforce only to hinder motivation. Furthermore, it hampers development at the lower levels and effectiveness at the higher.

> [F]oreign affiliates generally pay more – often substantially more – at general employee and *buchô* levels. But in the *kakarichô* and *kachô* grades of lower management, salaries paid by foreign affiliates are often lower than those at large Japanese firms.... [T]his pattern reflects the importance attached by foreign firms to managers at *buchô* level, whereas in Japanese firms the focus of organizing and directing work lies at the lower level – that of *kachô*. The salary disadvantage of lower management is aggravated by the fact that promotion from general employee to *kakarichô* also means the end of overtime pay. (IIBC 1987: 14)

If all that attracted the mid-career hired manager was the higher salary he would find it difficult to be accepted by the rest of the staff. Under these circumstances, if he were indeed offered an even higher salary elsewhere, namely by another foreign firm, it would be equally tempting.

Unfortunately, too few foreign firms pay attention to the participation of their Japanese managers in the mainstream of Japanese business, particularly in business organizations and training opportunities. Moreover, expatriate executives deficient in language skills tend to restrict their contacts with local staff to upper managers, who may then be evaluated for their ability to speak English or for such Western-style attitudes as assertiveness and aggressiveness, rather than for job performance. For the Japanese manager in a foreign firm, his major concern is whether his performance will be appraised according to Japanese or foreign standards. At the lower levels of the organization, the system of evaluation follows the Japanese pattern and usually does not present a problem, unless an expatriate manager becomes involved and the conclusion is influenced by the weaknesses in cross-cultural interaction.

> The Western approach to performance appraisals is often unsystematic but explicit, in contrast to the more implicit but systematic approach favored by the Japanese. Appraisals in the West are less frequent than is customary in Japan. In most cases, performance reviews are conducted annually, as opposed to the Japanese practice of having at least two or three reviews per year.... In Japanese firms, the appraisal standards and process are enforced vigorously at all levels of the organization, while in Western firms, individual

managers retain considerable freedom of action. (Pucik 1988: 492)

In Japanese firms a manager is not judged as if he were a specialist who performed a specific job satisfactorily in the period just before an appraisal; he is evaluated as a generalist whose *potential* is tested by measuring the contributions he has made over the years and how he is now appreciated by his peers and subordinates. Foreign firms also try to retain the Japanese manager who maintains high performance rather than the individual with average skills who may have found a cosy niche in the company. If a highly qualified mid-career performer fills a key slot in a long-term plan, his acceptance by the staff is greatly increased, which then enables him to stimulate motivation and work towards improving performance in a congenial environment.

7 Decision-making

With the standard style of corporate organization in Japan being organic, the corporate structure is such that it does not need to contend with narrowing the gap between decisions made by upper management and how they are implemented at lower levels. In a mechanistic organization, upper management is the first to assess the conditions of the surrounding environment and their reactions are then relayed to middle and lower management. The organic organization prefers to *absorb* reality by becoming a part of its environment, and its survival depends on how it perceives real conditions. The reality is a Japan under *modification*, where various shocks threaten the survival of its economy, its companies and its human resources. Rather than a concept or a topic controlled by the discussions of upper management, information relating to this reality has a more visceral form. Taking into account the complexities in internal and external circumstances, this instinctive mode is crucial to the organization at all levels. The life-expectancy of the corporate organism is limited by the subjective qualities of its human resources, which are defined by the diverse personalities, individual expectations, human relations, factions, etc. converging at a specific time and place.

The Western decision-making process with its clear implication on choice can be described in two linear steps:

$$\text{decision} \rightarrow \text{implementation}$$

On the other hand, the Japanese model can be expressed as a one-step circular process:

$$\text{necessity} = \text{performance}$$

Making a choice, i.e. a decision, is different from reacting in response to necessity, which is based on the idea of *learning by doing*. The practicality behind this realism is reinforced by two observations: first, no decision ever changes reality unless it is executed; and second, no decision can ever be changed; only a *new* decision can be made.

The Japanese manager is thus more interested in the implementation of a decision over the rationality of the decision. In other words, he does not try to change reality but is concerned with preparing the organization in *re*-acting to the impact of reality. After all, survival is the organic organization's priority.

The linear process of pursuing a problem and its possible solutions is a conceptual exercise, much as a traveller studies a map in order to reach his destination. Before starting on his journey he conceptualizes getting from point A to point B, hopefully selecting the right road to his destination. On the other hand, the circular process is specifically concerned with the journey so far as the territory itself is concerned; real dimensions are part of the exercise. The map can show the traveller how to reach his destination but it cannot take him there; he reaches his destination by crossing the given terrain and surviving its conditions. The circular process emphasizes performance, with destination automatically implying geography.

The circular process is reflected in the following characteristics of decision-making in Japanese industry.

1 Decision-making is not viewed as being regulated by corporate policy; it is internalized in the network of information that extends to all members of the organization. Less concern is given to the flow of authority, and more concern to the flow of work. Rather than the mere implementation of procedures and techniques, it is the involvement of people which makes the difference. A wider range of skills deepening individual experience and the perceived relevance of on-site knowledge by the workgroup permit almost full delegation of operational problem-solving. The ultimate safeguard, also the major motivation, is that the employee acts not in an individual capacity but as a member of a work team.

2 The overall process itself is more meaningful than the outcome, because emphasis is given to performance, where necessity determines what course of action is to be taken. The process is based more on actuality than conceptuality in the sense that decision (a conceptual step) and performance (an actual step) are understood as one move. Rather than the decision-maker and the decision, success depends on performance, i.e. on those who transform decisions into actual results.

As regards empirical decisions (i.e. those based on experience and information), minor decisions are made by less experienced managers (subordinates) while major decisions are made by more experienced managers (seniors). Subordinates' tentative decisions are formalized by seniors' approval. In the course of sharing responsibility with their subordinates, senior members can get information on the current situation or environment from subordinates, and adjust their past practices to a changing society. Subordinates, on the other hand, can reciprocally benefit from the seniors' past experience. Seniors have learned in their long employment that the training of subordinates is a key to the successful functioning of their divisions when they reach a more senior position. This vertical relationship not only provides effective continuity in corporate culture and reduces loss and risk, but also gives rational incentives to both seniors and their subordinates. Decisions that cannot be based on experience must be understood by all levels of members as fully as possible in order to be categorized as empirical decisions the next time. (Watanabe and Mochizuki 1986: 92)

3 Carrying out a decision places demands on the entire organization, which means that in order for everyone to be adequately equipped it is imperative that everyone be well-informed. And in this case it is information gained by participation that maintains a competent staff. Information is not hierarchically distributed within the company according to predetermined levels of confidentiality but is commonly shared through the intuition developed from working together over the years. In fact, both superiors and subordinates are on the same wavelength.

A decentralized approach to decision-making is seen to work best under routine operations that are basically stable and relatively predictable. The system, however, appears ill-suited to handle emergencies, unless the CEO at the executive level or the manager at the departmental level is willing to call on crisis management. But the manager does not need to wait for an emergency or turn to authority to take some course of action. As a matter concerning his own entrepreneurial leadership, he *pushes* (Chapter 6) in the direction that he believes will promote the survival of the organism.

The linear process represents a mechanistic style of corporate organization and may be superior in speed and efficiency while being backed by authority at any given stage. In contrast, the circular process characterizes the organic type of organization, giving it a major advantage in motivating the *actors*. And this may, in the end, be more effective.

IMPLEMENTING THE 'DECISION'

The process of promoting implementation in a circular fashion has been described in many ways. It has been defined as decision-making by *consensus*, but the term consensus is not to be taken from the view of a conceptual agreement, where participants simply agree on what is the *right* decision. Here, consensus means that participants keep abreast of the execution as it is being implemented, whether conceptually they agree with the *decision* or not. The process is also called *ringi-sei*, which refers to the practice of circulating a document (*ringi-sho*) often used in expediting an administrative assignment and recording approval. The Japanese prefer to use the term *nemawashi* to convey that information must be acquired by continuous participation in the flow of information. Meetings, both formal and informal, are held 'not to thrash out differences of opinion but to piece together compromise solutions that everyone can live with. Every effort is made to avoid splitting into majority and minority factions so that all members can feel their views have been taken into account' (Takashina 1988: 51). After all, members must work together in facilitating implementation.

> In Japan, where the underlying assumption seems to be that all members of a group will be, or should be, of the same mind, the principle is that no decision can be made without the unanimous approval – and silence is taken to mean approval – of the members. This means that to avoid confrontation potential opposition must be dealt with even before formal deliberation takes place, a process known as *nemawashi* – laying the groundwork, drumming up support. (Ibid.: 50–1)

In order to understand the decision-making process, informal and formal stages in the process need to be clarified; they may not be successive and may be repetitive. *Nemawashi* and *uchi-awase* are informal; *kaigi* and the circulation of the *ringi-sho* are formal. (Unfortunately, the full meaning of these Japanese terms is difficult to translate into the English language.)

Nemawashi

This term was originally used to describe a gardening technique. According to the *Kôjien* dictionary it means 'digging around the root of a big tree one or two years before its scheduled transplantation, and clipping off all but the main root and the large branch-roots and allowing new root hairs to grow, thus facilitating the transplantation, and also enabling the tree to bear better fruit'. The term has been adopted in all forms of decision-making, in political circles, administrative agencies, corporate organizations, and even in labour unions, as the example below shows.

> Since decisions of the legislative councils [in labour unions] are by consensus or majority vote, the top leaders must engage in various political maneuvers to obtain majority support. The executive officers are weak in statutory rights and duties, and decisions are made collectively; hence it is essential that the officers retain the support of their trusted factions and caucuses. If the leader's faction does not command a stable majority, he must negotiate with other factions, even those in overt opposition, in order to move the convention in the desired direction. Hence, *nemawashi* is carried out prior to the formal debate and vote. In many cases, the formal decision on the floor is little more than a ceremony to confirm the decision already reached behind closed doors. In such cases, decision-making is done in places and through procedures totally unknown to the rank-and-file union member. Great ability or wisdom in such political maneuvers is one of the most important qualities of a union leader. (Quoted in Matsumoto 1984: 95)

In the corporate context, *nemawashi* is used behind the scenes as a preliminary step in the decision-making process. Once a proposal is submitted, those who may influence its acceptance will invariably be approached on an individual basis. In order to gain support, informal contact is needed to explain the ideas behind the proposal as well as seek out the opinions of others in a subtle way. *Nemawashi* may seem quite routine but it is rather time-consuming, depending on the complexity of the matter and other factors such as the presence of conflicting factions. However, more than the matter under review it is the process, *nemawashi* itself, that is the main point.

Uchi-awase

At first glance, *uchi-awase* is not clearly distinguishable from *nemawashi*. However, *nemawashi* tends to be more subjective in style,

while *uchi-awase* is concerned with the concrete details of implementation in terms of the participants involved and the resources
needed, much like a working session would be. *Uchi-awase* can also
be arranged in the form of a social gathering, an informal meeting of
the individuals involved in *nemawashi* who will participate in the
kaigi (formal conference). In this form, the opinions gathered
through *nemawashi* are pooled to establish some common objectives
for the proposal. Both types of meetings often take place in a
teahouse or on the golf course, but also during lunch hours or a
favourite stopover on the way home from work. The more complex
or politicized the problem, the greater the importance and the longer
the time given to *nemawashi* and *uchi-awase*.

Kaigi

Nemawashi and *uchi-awase* attempt to coordinate interrelated activities and often involve bargaining among various functional units of
the organization. They share the common purpose of assuming
responsibility in implementation. But at some point, a consensus for
action beyond the physical aspects of the project will need to be made
more explicit. This becomes the focus of the different *kaigi* that are
normally scheduled to allow managers (department heads, section
chiefs, etc.) to meet on a regular basis. The *kaigi* is a formal conference but it does not need to debate over the conceptual aspects of a
decision, since this should have been completed at the stages of
nemawashi and *uchi-awase*. Rather, it is chiefly concerned with
increasing the general awareness of the current *situation*. The expression *matomari* (pulling the threads together) can be used to explain
the idea behind the *kaigi*. If this is not achieved the decision may be
delayed until some compromise can be reached.

Ringi-sho

Usually, when a *kaigi* is successfully concluded it is followed up by a
ringi-sho, a detailed proposal directly related to implementation.
Serving as an instrument of approval and administrative assignment,
the document also acts as a convenient record.

This decision-making process can be illustrated as in Figure 7.1,
showing the three levels of corporate structure, i.e. *keiei-sha, kanri-
sha,* and *ippan sha-in,* and the human resources that support each
level, (see Appendix II, which describes how a major electronics
manufacturer decides on the construction of a new factory).

Figure 7.1 Japanese corporate structure and the decision-making process

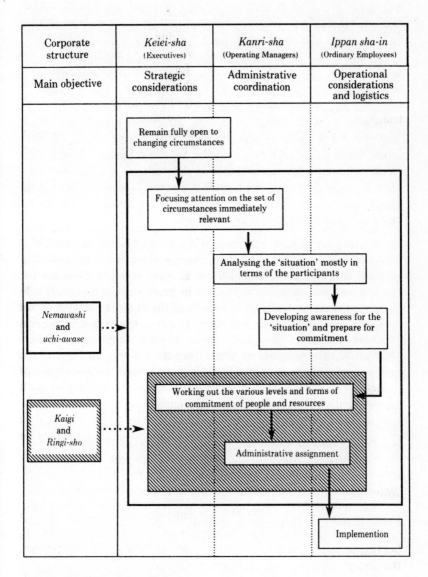

Source: Inspired by Hattori 1978: 14

IN FOREIGN FIRMS

Decision-making in foreign firms is simply based on 'who decides is not who executes and *vice versa*'. Control is essential to the foreign investor because control is equated with the capacity to make decisions. But the negative effects of this kind of mentality are evident in international joint ventures, which were thought to be the solution to the problem of doing business in Japan. Ironically, the real obstacle many of them faced often turned out to be in the joint venture itself, where the foreign partner (under the direction of the home office) negotiated a position of majority control in order to make the decisions, leaving implementation to the Japanese partner. It may be a Western idiosyncrasy to believe that the decision is more important than its implementation; the trouble is that the Japanese believe in the exact opposite, in which case the chances for developing a fruitful partnership are indeed at a disadvantage.

> The mission of joint ventures, in the view of many partners, is to do what they are told by their parents. But, like baby birds that grow up and fly away from the nest, joint ventures often head in their own direction. Those that are given enough leeway frequently have lessons to teach their founders. Three prominent examples are Nippon Otis, Fuji Xerox, and Yokogawa-Hewlett-Packard. These companies struggled hard to get their American parents to listen to their suggestions about cooperation and quality control. Their persistence benefited both them and their creators. (Goldenberg 1988: 225)

The split between decision and implementation may be worse in subsidiaries that are wholly owned by the foreign investor, where the local staff often complain that the foreign side readily takes the credit for any success, which in the eyes of the foreign staff is directly related to the decisions they made, whereas in the event of failure the Japanese staff may be blamed for some faultiness in implementation.

Whether conflicts such as these can be solved by consultation between the opposing sides is open to question; consultation may be *pro forma* unless the decision and its implementation can be examined together. Granting the difficulty foreign firms have in relating to their local personnel, one would expect that consultation would be better off if left to the Japanese themselves. A survey of labour–management relations in foreign firms conducted by the Ministry of Labour assessed the different degrees of *consultation* between foreign and Japanese executives on matters relating to personnel and labour, such as activity plans, organization, the wage system, promotion, dismissal, etc. Generally speaking, the higher the foreign capital ratio the larger the direct foreign control and the concern for consultation. The proportion of Japanese control rises when the ratio of foreign capital falls, the period of establishment in Japan lengthens, or the local workforce expands (MOL 1988b: 118–23). From these observations it appears that decision by so-called consultation is essentially a means of control.

Concerning foreign operations in Japan, a common observation made among expatriate executives is that during meetings called to debate on a major decision, their Japanese counterparts are reluctant to verbalize their views. The Japanese tend to avoid the practice of open debate, since it is considered to be socially unacceptable. In fact, the foreigner is likely to get the impression that they have already made up their minds beforehand. Although this is most likely the case, the trouble is that the foreign side was not involved in, probably not even aware of, the *nemawashi* that took place. On the other hand, the expatriate manager and those at the home office feel ill-at-ease with the Japanese style of decision-making. Wanting to discuss problems and solutions to reach a decision, the manager is always anxious to argue for the rationality of his views, while his Japanese counterparts prefer to discuss the problem in private, loathing open argumentation, and saving their energy for implementation.

In the wholly owned subsidiary a distinction is often made between strategic and operational decisions. The latter are generally delegated to the executives on the spot, whether expatriate or Japanese. Making strategic decisions requires constructive support, which the expatriate executive can manage to marshal at the home office, but what about their immediate execution? Foreign businessmen complain that the Japanese take an indefinite amount of time to reach a decision (though they do tend to move swiftly once a decision is made). The Japanese view that foreign executives are indeed quick at reaching decisions, but that implementation does not necessarily follow.

The lack (or neglect) of understanding for the Japanese style of decision-making is clearly manifested in the attitude presented by the foreign businessman who wants a decision immediately and thus approaches 'decision' makers. It would be more effective (and perhaps more efficient) to pay a courtesy visit to the company president and let those under him worry about the execution of what is being proposed. The same applies when dealing with government offices. The matter on hand should first be cleared with the junior staff, since they do have significant discretionary authority. Without some urgent reason, the senior staff will rarely override the *decisions* taken by subordinates.

APPENDIX II

CASE STUDY: THE CONSTRUCTION OF A NEW FACTORY

At one of the largest Japanese electronics manufacturers the decision to construct a new factory took about 24 months. The decision materialized in the following way.

Months 1–3:

The general manager of the Product Division, sensing a need for an additional factory through his daily contacts with his department managers and encouraged by hints provided by some managers in the Field Sales Department, makes up his mind that the time had come to pursue his objective. He starts the *nemawashi* process by mentioning it offhand to the managers in his division.

Months 3–6:

Nemawashi now spreads to those at the Corporate Staff level. (In this company, corporate staff includes those in corporate planning, personnel, finance and accounting, marketing, engineering and production control.) The general manager, on his own initiative, mentions his objective to one of the senior directors, who happens to be a personal acquaintance, and the senior director reacts positively.

Months 6–12:

While *nemawashi* continues unabated, *uchi-awase* is taking place. The 'idea' of a new factory is brought up in various circles. Frequent *uchi-awase* are held between production managers, field sales managers and some of their subordinates. After checking with the Corporate Staff (with personnel in particular) and informally with several directors (the senior director 'acquaintance' had already informed the president), the man chosen to be the manager of the proposed factory begins to participate in these working sessions from about month 10 onwards.

Months 12–18:

More *uchi-awase*, on the basis of more *nemawashi*, takes place with the managers of other divisions, mostly upon the initiative of the Production managers. Finally, Production managers, with the help of the Finance and Accounting Department (Corporate Staff level), organize everything in the form of a draft plan in order to control the focus of the discussions.

Figure 7.2 Schematic flow of decision-making: new factory construction case study

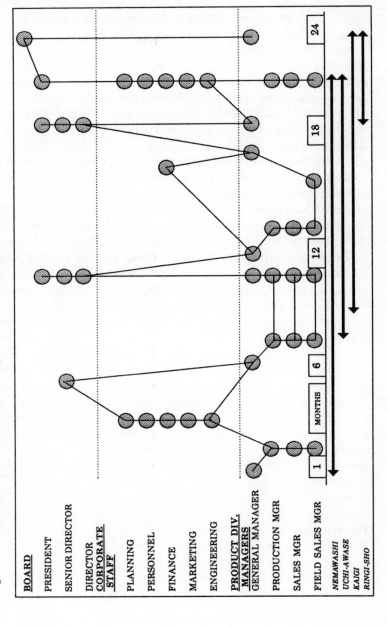

Months 18–21:

The draft is further discussed with the general manager, Corporate Staff and some directors, and the plan is repeatedly brought up in regular managers' *kaigi.* The directors then appoint the general manager to the duty of circulating the *ringi-sho.* He explains everything in detail to one of his subordinates, who writes it up in the proper form of a *ringi-sho.*

Months 18–21:

The *ringi-sho* is formally circulated to all departments of the Product Division and to the heads of some other divisions, then continues on up to the Corporate Staff and is finally submitted to and endorsed by the Board of Directors.

Months 23–24:

Finalizing blueprints takes two more months. (There is no need for bidding since, as is commonly the practice, the company turns to the building contractor that previously handled construction in that region. In fact, from about month 12, this contractor had participated in many of the *uchi-awase.*) By the end of month 24, bulldozers move on to the site.

Graphically expressed, the path of this process (limited to the Division concerned) can be traced as in Figure 7.2.

Part III
The marketplace

When the Japanese company enters the marketplace it can count on the total commitment of its corporate members (*sha-in*) to make it a success. But so do its competitors, creating a competition in the domestic market that is indeed fierce. None the less, a company cannot survive on its own. Each company builds its own network of support whereby suppliers, distributors and even users are expected to act as its allies, which makes the competition even tougher. Business transactions, as everything else in Japanese society, emphasize the long-term relationship, as exemplified by the current practice of subcontracting. As a direct consequence, producers, vendors, distribution channels, and oftentimes the clientele in new product development depend on Total Quality Control (TQC). Thus, establishing and maintaining this network becomes a crucial factor in determining survival in the marketplace.

Foreign firms cannot escape the subjectivity inherent in their own human resources and as such must adjust to the interaction of other human values as they exist in the product and service markets. Operations in Japan are required in order to compete in Japan, but that is not enough. A sophisticated corporate presence that can readily apply patience and experience to whatever situation is at hand is an investment that needs to be made.

8 Business transactions

Business transactions in Japan are concerned with more than just the commercial aspect, and so the idea of dealing at arm's length is rather incomprehensible to large companies and even more so to small firms. A business practice attesting to this that happens to be particularly widespread is the so-called *kankei-gaisha* (related companies); here, interests go beyond just owning a controlling interest in another company. Basically, a Japanese entrepreneur who establishes *related* companies chooses to do so for managerial, personnel and financial reasons (Ballon and Tomita 1988: 38–42).

From the viewpoint of corporate management, establishing an autonomous entity that is separately managed is sometimes preferred to branching out into a new type of business as a part of the same company. Thus it is common to see a wholly owned trading subsidiary handling all sales of the parent manufacturer. The joint venture subsidiary is seen to be a convenient alternative in the case when foreign technology and knowhow cannot be obtained on a straight licensing basis.

In the area of personnel, it is a common as well as convenient practice to transfer redundant managerial staff to related companies. And considering that under enterprise unionism ('one company, one union') the same employment conditions apply to all union members that belong to the same company regardless of differing work circumstances, establishing a new corporate entity with new employment regulations may be a reasonable step to take.

As to the financial advantage, if the subsidiary is a minority shareholder of the parent the capital contribution to the latter expands, which reinforces the stability of the shareholder. Intercompany sales and purchases can benefit as well. Loans and trade credit from financial institutions are in some cases larger when granted to plural entities than to a single entity, and intercompany guarantees can be obtained on loans (often left unreported in financial statements). Subsidiaries also have some tax advantages. And the subsidiary can be used to smooth profits of the parent company by adjusting the prices used in intercompany dealings, even through unrealized sales and flexible financial period endings.

With the *kankei-gaisha*, along with most (if not all) Japanese companies, business transactions are not any different from the interaction we find among the Japanese themselves. As in dealing with any human relationship, a considerable degree of subjectivity is involved, which greatly contrasts with the cool legal objectivity of the contract.

CONTRACT

Under the Western legal tradition, the business contract respects the autonomy of each party only as qualified by the conditions of the contract. Everything is dependent on documentation, where power resides in the written word and the use of courts or arbitrators is accepted as a natural part of the process. Western law was introduced into Japan about a century ago, but the traditional way of contracting based on social relationships is still preferred. Emphasis is placed on human interaction, which means that conflicts are usually dealt with by consulting among the parties involved and, if necessary, conciliating with third parties presiding.

Japanese lawyers and judges do not play a very prominent role, except in cases where international contracts are involved which need to be dealt with according to Western legal principles. That major Japanese corporations began to establish the equivalent of a Legal Department at their head offices is a rather recent phenomenon. In most cases, this department originates back to the late 1960s, when companies started to react to pressures arising from issues such as: the pollution problems created by the unchecked industrial expansion propelled by the high rate of economic growth; the advent of consumer movements aided by the growing authority of the Fair Trade Commission (the administrative branch of the postwar antimonopoly legislation); and the growing involvement of Japan, first in international trade and then in overseas direct investment.

Legal matters are usually handled by the Legal section (*hômu-ka*), which is itself a part of the General Affairs department (*sômu-bu*). Many companies avoid the terms *Hôki-ka* or *Hômu-ka* (legal section) in referring to this section, since it lends the appearance of being overly legalistic. *Bunsho-ka* (archive section) is preferred to these. This legal section, even in the largest companies, is composed not of professional lawyers but of regular employees who have learned how to handle corporate legal practice through experience gained while working at the company. Theoretically, it would be expected to review contracts, coordinate litigation and outside attorneys, be entrusted with industrial and other legislation related to the company, keep an eye on legal developments, and instruct the staff on matters pertaining to the law. In practice, though, these responsibilities are assumed by other departments (Ballon 1988: 14–19). Consequently, Japanese companies are not dependent upon legal professionals, be they attorneys-at-law or judges.

> Japanese not only hesitate to resort to a lawsuit but are also quite ready to settle an action already instituted through conciliatory processes during the course of litigation. With this inclination in the background, judges are likely to hesitate, or at least not seek, to expedite judicial decisions, preferring instead to reconcile the litigant parties.... Complaint about delay in reaching judicial decisions is almost universal, particularly in recent years, and the reasons for the delay are diverse. But one reason may be this judicial hesitancy to attribute clear-cut victory and defeat to the respective parties.... Furthermore, it seems that judges are rather commonly inclined to attach importance to the status quo or to a *fait accompli* .... Considering these facts, parties in a dispute usually find that resort to a lawsuit is less profitable than resort to other means of settlement. (Tanaka 1976: 283–4)

Contracts customarily used among Japanese companies are drawn up in a tone which contrasts sharply with what the West sees as legal and professional. For example, in contracts between Japanese companies,

- The wording is not lengthy, detailed or specific; it is concise, general and open-ended. At the time of negotiations, and later when deliberations are held, there is always room for playing up *tatemae/honne* (what is externally expressed/what is internally thought).
- No clause of the contract is negotiated or decided just on its own merits; each is considered as one part of the organic whole, represented in this case by the relationship of the contracting parties. This relationship determines how successfully a contract will be carried out.
- The document *per se* is not regarded as the limits within which the performance must be carried out, or as a possible tool to use in

court; it is taken more as a record of negotiations that shows a relationship was recognized and given a chance to grow.
– A change in circumstance tests not so much the validity of the contract, but the durability of the relationship.

A standard contract between two Japanese companies is two or three pages long and contains about a dozen articles. The agreement is purposely not made in detailed terms so that the flexibility deemed as indispensable for satisfactory performance is not restricted. The final clause apparently throws all caution to the winds: *Concerning matters not stipulated herein or any doubt about the stipulation, both parties shall settle them upon deliberation.* Both parties recognize the need to make adjustments in obligations, but the manner in which to propose any changes appears limited to consultation. (An example of a typical Japanese-style contract is given in Appendix III.)

An exception to the above is the Agreement on Bank Transactions that every customer is expected to sign on unilateral terms in favour of the bank. However, the general understanding is that

> [T]he terms and conditions contained in the Agreement on Bank Transactions and the related agreements submitted by a bank's customer in connection with the Agreement on Bank Transactions, are not strictly enforced so long as the relationship between the customer and the bank is generally good. Practically speaking, disputes or misunderstandings between a bank and its customers are settled through the custom of trade or mutually amicable discussions, regardless of the actual terms and conditions contained in the Agreement on Bank Transactions and the other related documents. (Oda and Grice 1988: 25–6)

In dealing with business transactions, Japanese companies adhere to tradition as they continue to invest in a relationship that builds on two interrelated factors: a long-term view that forms the basis of the relationship, and the belief that changing circumstances give the relationship its vitality.

RELATIONSHIP

The Japanese business transaction is more than a temporary arrangement between the independent parties agreeing to certain conditions and outcomes: in the eyes of the Japanese it has established an interdependence among all contracting parties. Since the outcome is subject to the relationships that fulfil the contractual obligations, the human dimension in carrying out the contract is of the utmost significance. The explanation used in Chapter 3 can be used again to highlight the difference between the two:

Contract	$(1 + 1 = 2)$
Relationship	$(1 \times 1 = 1)$

The contract $(1 + 1 = 2)$ reflects the pattern where both parties essentially maintain their independence but agree to cooperate in *contracted* areas without encroaching upon each other's separate identities. It indicates a Western pattern, where rights and obligations are expected to be mutually recognized by acting in accordance with the stipulations of the contract. Seen as a relationship $(1 \times 1 = 1)$, the pattern which emerges shows that the independence of the contracting parties has been replaced by interdependence. Emphasis is put on the dynamic quality of harmony (*wa*) but it is never taken for granted, since it can only be generated by constant interaction. Not only can more benefits be expected from the relationship (over an indefinite period) than from the contract (over a set period), but the difficulties are greater as well. As illustrated by Figure 8.1, the contract covers only the portion where the parties involved overlap, but the relationship absorbs all parties in their entirety.

The best examples of the *relationship* are found in subcontracting (Ballon 1989). The Fair Trade Commission (FTC) surveyed the user-supplier relationship of 200 large, non-financial companies, out of which 94 responded. With regard to both producer goods and capital goods, an overwhelming number responded that they had a long-term relationship with all or a majority of their suppliers, experiencing little turnover in the last three years (FTC 1987: 17). A practical way of conducting business, it has many advantages.

> A close, long-term relationship with a few suppliers affords substantial reductions in supplier management costs as suppliers can be increasingly relied on to perform product inspections and inventory control, to protect technical secrets, and to settle transactions smoothly. In a long-term relationship, communication becomes simpler and mutual understanding develops; this is seen as a major advantage in purchasing from existing suppliers.... Even when a competitor offers a 10 per cent discount, existing suppliers will immediately match the discount. In contrast, in America, a 10 per cent price difference would often produce a change in suppliers. (FTC 1987: 8 and 12)

Figure 8.1 The Western contract and the Japanese relationship

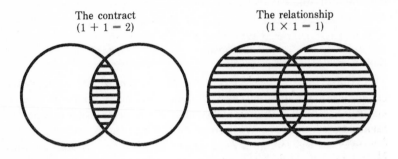

The contract
(1 + 1 = 2)

The relationship
(1 × 1 = 1)

The subcontracting relationship thrives on much subjectivity as, in the first place, it manifests a preference for long term, ongoing relationships and thus chooses to deal with a limited number of firms when placing or filling orders, all regulated through tacit understanding rather than documented contracts, and, in the second place, the core firm pays close attention to the quality of management when selecting subcontractors, who relinquish some control of their internal management in the hope of sharing in the benefits of growth. When asked about the reasons for maintaining a long-term relationship, Japanese managers make it clear that open bidding is not a satisfactory method by stressing risk-sharing, in quality, delivery and pricing (Table 8.1). All in all, interdependence at its best.

Japanese manufacturers have been trying to implement the long-term view in their plants abroad, as shown by Honda's relationship with its supplier Capitol in the United States. The following is a view from the supplier's side.

'... [B]efore an order was placed, a team of purchasing people visited us in Bowling Green to inspect and review everything. I estimate that 150 people must have come through here, including some Japanese directors from Honda Motor Company. While their requests seemed unusual to us, we turned over everything they wanted to examine. For instance, they asked to see a detailed cost breakdown of our proposals. In the past, other manufacturers only looked at the bottom line, not how we got there.... With this information, they'd come back and make suggestion after suggestion on ways we could improve....' Taylor [Capitol's president] estimates that it was nearly three years after Capitol's first contact with Honda before the first order was placed .... The first shipment

Table 8.1 Reasons for long-term user–supplier relationship, 1986 (per cent of respondents, multiple answers)

Reasons	Producer goods	Capital goods
Better quality	73.3	82.4
Ensure security of supply	88.4	44.0
Better prices	50.0	53.8
Proven reliability	47.7	46.2
Short delivery period	7.0	18.7
Supplier's adaptability, flexibility	5.8	13.2
Same industrial group	8.1	5.5
Joint development projects	5.8	2.2
Major purchaser of finished products	4.7	3.3
Sole source of supply	1.2	5.5
Favourable terms (other than payment)	4.7	7.7
Favourable payment terms	–	2.2
Others	1.2	4.4

Source: FTC 1987: 18

carried an invoice for $238. 'If I were to put a dollar value on the human hours of engineering time, sales proposals, management meetings, and so on, we probably invested $200,000 to get that first order....' According to Taylor, Capitol and Honda today have an unusual rapport that resembles a partnership more than a seller–customer relationship. (Shook 1988: 178–9)

Toshiba Consumer Products Ltd (TPC) took up a similar effort at integrating suppliers in the United Kingdom.

They [suppliers] find that the messages about quality and cost reduction come over loud and clear at the suppliers' conferences but they appreciate several things about the meetings. The first is that they are held at all. One supplier remarked that he 'couldn't think of a single UK firm' that held anything like them. In spite of 'TCP propaganda', suppliers can put [in] their point of view and can have a two-way discussion. TCP does inform them in advance of its plans and does visit them to discuss problems that may arise with items *before* they go into production: a way of trying to prevent problems arising that was not said to be characteristic of British customers. Suppliers appreciated TCP's disclosure of information at the conferences and when requested in the course of business, although reciprocal openness regarding quotations, for instance, was also expected. Here again, the type and amount of information exchanged was greater than with British companies. TCP was seen to be demanding high standards of quality and delivery and keen pricing but also to be willing to work together with suppliers to overcome technical difficulties. The point about the long-term philosophy seemed to have got across and that TCP would persevere with a supplier to solve the problems and only break off relations if the situation finally appeared beyond help. This was said to contrast with the attitude of British companies, whose relations with suppliers were remote and who would let the supplier sink or swim on his own, dropping him at short notice. (Trevor 1988: 155–6)

CHANGING CIRCUMSTANCES

The contract clearly indicates a time frame, but even within the set period circumstances are not assumed to remain without change. In the West, supervening events are supposedly covered by legal theory and practice. However, the Japanese businessman believes that since the future is unforeseeable, the circumstances under which a contract is negotiated are unpredictable. Flexibility in carrying out the contract is taken for granted as circumstances are interpreted in the wider context of the relationship. Way before the contract is even signed, negotiations have not only determined the details of fulfilling the contract, but the personalities of the parties involved have also been studied to help them deal on better terms (Kester 1991: 62–7). The phrases *upon deliberation* and *in good faith* appear repeatedly in the contract, serving to remind the parties of all previous negotiations in which they have thus far participated.

Supervening events often make the party feel trapped by the contract and the only solution seems to be to look for a way out. The Westerner may choose litigation because this is an accepted procedure in his culture. But the Japanese is much less likely to do so, not necessarily because he is less litigious by nature, but because his culture restricts him with other means of social control. In fact, one of the reasons why Japanese companies prefer a select circle of suppliers is to control those who might take advantage of the situation.

[A] business may choose to keep its activities within a circumscribed group in which information about the other contracting party is readily available and in which public sanctions against opportunistic behavior exist. Consider the Japanese penchant for introductions. Many Japanese businesses, including law firms, will deal only with parties that can submit introductions from respected third parties. The introduction verifies both that the party has acted in ways considered 'honorable' within the universe of 'reputable' businesses and that it will be subject to the sanctions of the third party if it tries to act 'dishonorably' in the future. The loosely organized Japanese conglomerates fulfill a similar function. When a member of a conglomerate contracts with another member of the group, it contracts with a firm about which it has extensive information and does so with little risk that the firm will not honor the terms of the contract. The more a business limits its deals to contracts with a universe of firms subscribing to a common code of honorable behavior and subject to the sanctions of others within this universe, the less cost-effective an investment in contractual draftsmanship becomes. (Ramseyer 1986: 521–2)

Such an indifferent view of legal precautions stems from the widely held assumption that conflict should be avoided. If conflict does occur it should be settled not by litigation but through dialogue. Japanese legal experts have pointed out that Japanese contracts 'do not provide criteria which can be applied to all possible disagreements. Instead, they express a general policy of settling disputes by mutual understanding' (Hanami 1979: 53). In fact, apology is the accustomed way of recognizing and revitalizing the human relationship in public and private life, which thus cannot help but influence contractual relations (Wagatsuma and Rosett 1986). The aim is to dispel the chances of a dispute occurring, to the extent that an outsider could take the underlying motive as simply to ignore any signs of dispute. The idea is expressed by the Japanese proverb: *Arasoi wo mizu ni nagasu*, 'let the dispute flow out with the water'. The legal contract is only a record of the transaction. It depends on the relationship to come to life as well as to solve whatever conflict that may arise. 'Law in Japan is like an heirloom samurai sword; it is to be treasured but not used' (quoted by Haley 1982: 265).

When a dispute arises between two parties, not very many Japanese view the dispute in terms of rights and obligations. Nor does it occur to them when they fail to work out a solution between themselves that the best approach to the dispute is to take the matter to court. Instead, the traditional value of 'harmony' (*wa*) prevails upon them. To their minds, settlement of disputes without arguing their points of view in a reasoned way and without fighting out their cases to the finish in court, is a supreme virtue. (Compromise in the political world is another manifestation of this spirit. In reaching a political compromise, Japanese often shelve their principles and work out a compromise by 'adding their contentions and dividing the sum by two.') The traditional spirit of harmony, however, does not inculcate a concept of settlement based on a reasoned compromise between the parties incorporating a clear notion of one's rights. By the same token, only in a very small number of instances is a detailed arrangement made between the parties in advance for the purpose of preventing disputes arising later. (Tanaka 1976: 261)

IN FOREIGN FIRMS

The foreign firm in Japan may, without justification, interpret the subjectivity that it finds rooted in business relations among the local firms as a general reluctance to purchase foreign products. Western businessmen react to this unfamiliar environment by resorting to the more tangible safeguards found in the Western legal tradition, even though they themselves may conduct much of their business without contract back in their own countries. But, in Japan, legal recourse is not the solution, except perhaps in industrial property cases. Of course, there is no business without some degree of trust, but the foreign firm supposes that trust is more easily gained with a carefully drafted contract. The problem is that the prevailing Japanese custom is to pay less attention to the contract itself.

Most contract difficulties faced by the foreign firm are not visible on a day-to-day basis but surface when it maintains a long-term relationship as supplier or as partner.

As supplier

Not infrequently, foreign firms in Japan provide goods and services to local interests without a written contract. The experience of a major oil company shows how insignificant a contract can be.

Shell operating in Japan for over 80 years had no written contract with its dealers for the first 60 years! When a contract form was devised under strong advice of the lawyers, and sent out to dealers for their signature, the action surprised the over one thousand dealers throughout the country. They considered such formality as unnecessary, and after sending back the signed form as requested, never referred to it afterwards. (Miyai 1985: 15)

The tendency for Westerners to depend on the contract and the accuracy of its wording is as strong as that of the Japanese to depend on negotiations and the *subjective* elements. In his observation of American sellers (equally applicable to Europeans), Graham presents the following view:

> Given the vertical relationships between Japanese negotiators and the more horizontal relationships typical of American negotiators, what happens in cross-cultural negotiations? It is my belief that a Japanese seller and an American buyer will get along fine, while the American seller and the Japanese buyer will have great problems.... When Japanese sellers come to the United States to market their products, they naturally assume the lower-status position and act accordingly (with great respect for the American buyer), and a sale is made. Initially, the Japanese sellers are taken advantage of. After all, they expected the American buyer to respect their needs.... But in any case, relationships are established between firms. The door is open and the Japanese sellers have the opportunity to learn the 'American way', to adjust their behavior, and to establish more viable long-term relationships.
>
> However, if American sellers take their normative set of bargaining behaviors to Japan, then negotiations are apt to end abruptly. The American seller expects to be treated as an equal and acts accordingly. The Japanese buyer is likely to view this rather brash behavior in a lower-status seller as inappropriate and lacking in respect. The Japanese buyer is made to feel uncomfortable and politely shuts the door to trade, without explanation. The American seller never makes the first sale and never gets an opportunity to learn the Japanese system. (Graham 1988: 484)

Even among themselves, the Japanese expect to receive many visits by the salesman before a deal is made, regardless of whether the client happens to be a large company or the local retail shop. The cultivation of the sales relationship, not the sales contract, is what is important. The following anecdote, which came up during a discussion with foreign businessmen, shows how effective the relationship can be. As a result of the sudden jump in oil prices in 1973, a large European chemical company faced the dilemma of not being able to supply a major Japanese client according to contract. The advice of the legal counsel at the home office was to cancel the contract and pay the appropriate damages in order to maintain a favourable long-term business relationship. Instructions to that effect were sent to the subsidiary in Japan. But the expatriate executive there who had been working many years in Japan thought otherwise. He recalled several instances where Japanese clients had brought up the matter of *changing circumstances* and proposed a new course of action, without the slightest reference to what contract stipulations were in force. Would it work the other way round, i.e. would the same considerations be given to the foreign company? Since the lowest estimate for damages was a 6-digit dollar figure, it was worth a try. It worked. The client's understanding resulted from the kind of relationship that existed. In fact, cooperation in solving the problem only served to enhance the relationship.

Here is another example of the supplier relationship, as reported by the president of Grace Japan K.K.:

> We are currently one of the three major suppliers of a certain chemical product to a top car manufacturer. It took three years to become a candidate supplier, in spite of the fact that we introduced a new product which no one was supplying. It took another year before finally being admitted to the select circle of chemical product suppliers. Although our product was a uniquely new material not available from existing suppliers, the car manufacturer decided, to our dismay, to give them the opportunity to meet our specifications, properties and characteristics in order not to disrupt a long standing relationship. Before final approval was given, a total of two dozen people, mainly technical, visited our plant at Atsugi on several occasions .... We were requested to present our policy on quality assurance, organization chart, quality assurance systems and procedures, manufacturing facilities, history of product development, manufacturing processes, inspection specifications, QC and quality improvement, etc .... There was no secret left. (Makino 1987: 8)

The foreign firm, or rather its home office, is critical of the reluctance the Japanese exhibit towards open bidding. But the Japanese justify their behaviour as merely preserving the long-term relationship, accepting the subjective aspects in order to enjoy the economic advantages. This is why they prefer the Just-in-Time delivery system (Chapter 9).

As partner

A substantial number of business contracts involving foreign firms are related to the international joint venture. It is seen as a type of business endeavour that is prone to friction between contract and relationship and it is often avoided under the pretext that it has outlived its usefulness. But a study sponsored by the American Chamber of Commerce in Japan and the Council of the European Business Community proves otherwise:

> The mail survey results indicate that the mutual basis for forming a joint venture is still similar to what it has traditionally been.... Forty-five per cent of the respondents listed technology as the number one contribution of the foreign partner to a joint venture, putting this far ahead of other contributions in terms of importance. The Japanese partner's most important contributions were split among personnel, sales and distribution, and management expertise. It is notable, however, that in 11 per cent of the cases technology was the number one contribution of the Japanese partner and in 14 per cent of the cases sales and distribution was the number one contribution of the foreign partner. This attests to the growing importance of Japanese technology and the growing trend toward joint ventures with Japanese companies for foreign markets. (Booz, Allen & Hamilton 1987: 27 and 29)

The problem is that all too often the partners, foreign as well as Japanese, find themselves wondering what the other party is up to. There is much more to the marketplace than what can be detailed in the basic agreement of the joint venture. It is easy to blame Japanese idiosyncracies when something goes wrong, but Western idiosyncracies are equally at fault (and surface as readily in the wholly owned subsidiary). The joint venture is often not an attractive choice for the foreign investor since he loses full control of operations. His key concern is to maintain as much effective control as possible. Equity participation is assumed to be *ipso facto* management participation, as if management and equity are measured by the same yardstick. However, experts on the subject have noted that '[t]he balance of equity in a venture – either foreign minority, 50–50, or foreign majority – is not by itself the critical factor in determining a venture's success or failure' (Abegglen and Stalk 1985: 228). The foreign investor should show more concern in the purpose of the joint venture, which in most cases means gaining access to the Japanese market in exchange for technological know-how or brand recognition. But whatever the focus of business, one key factor is often overlooked or taken for granted, namely the striking imbalance in their human resources. A typical profile of the joint venture partners in this respect can be outlined as:

Foreign investor	*Japanese investor*
Chairman	President
and some directors	and directors (often doubling
residing outside Japan	as operations managers)
+ (temporary) vice president	+ all managers
	+ all regular employees
	+ suppliers, distributors and
	customers

The advantage of joint ventures is that they can be used as an entry vehicle, and sometimes as a means of exit as well. In other words, once the foreign investor starts to learn about doing business in Japan according to Japanese rules, he can sell out to, or buy out, his Japanese partner.

A recent trend is the strategic alliance, for example in co-marketing and co-development, which seems to offer definite advantages for a wider and more rapid market penetration (Ohmae 1989). It is then vital for the foreign firm, especially its expatriate executives, to appreciate contract negotiations in Japanese terms.

> The Japanese approach to contract negotiations is that they are a kind of courtship intended to culminate, if successful, in the establishment of a long-term cooperation between the parties based not only on legal considerations but also on a spirit of mutual trust. Since the establishment of mutual trust requires some time, negotiations with Japanese companies are often extended and prolonged. Moreover, in Japanese companies, decisions are usually the product of extensive consultations with people and departments throughout the organization, not merely a few top-level executives. Negotiations will therefore involve many separate meetings over a long period of time and endless discussions of points seemingly already settled. Although the negotiations may be tiresome, the benefits of such a process are that once an agreement is signed, implementation will proceed relatively easily because understanding and support have been obtained from the entire organization of the company. (Matsushita and Schoenbaum 1989: 47)

APPENDIX III TYPICAL SALES CONTRACT BETWEEN TWO JAPANESE COMPANIES

The following is a typical sales contract between two Japanese companies, courtesy of the Legal Affairs Department of Nippon Light Metal, Ltd, as translated by E. Kanno.

NIPPON LIGHT METAL COMPANY, LTD. (hereinafter called X) and Y CHEMICAL COMPANY, LTD. (hereinafter called Y) agree as follows concerning the transactions of chemicals (hereinafter called CHEMICALS) which are enclosed in a metal container.

Article 1   Transaction of Chemicals
Y shall manufacture CHEMICALS on X's order, and X shall buy them.

Article 2   Limitation on Manufacturer and Sales
Y shall not sell CHEMICALS or same kind of CHEMICALS which will compete with CHEMICALS to a third party other than X without X's prior written consent.

X shall not buy CHEMICALS or same kind of CHEMICALS which will compete with CHEMICALS from a third party other than Y without Y's prior written consent.

Article 3   Individual Sales Contract
An individual transaction between X and Y shall be conducted by issuing an order sheet and a written acknowledgement thereof each time.

Article 4   Price
Prices of CHEMICALS shall be decided upon deliberation [emphasis added] between X and Y.

Article 5   Delivery
1. X shall designate the place and delivery date of CHEMICALS.
2. Delivery is deemed to be completed when X or X's agent designated by X hands in a receipt of CHEMICALS.
3. Y shall be relieved of its obligation as a seller when the delivery is finished. However, quality assurance shall be decided by a separate memorandum.
4. An examination by X shall be finished at the same time as the delivery of CHEMICALS. Further, X is entitled to request Y to submit necessary materials for the examination, and to cooperate with the test and check at the production line, and Y shall cooperate with this.
5. The title to CHEMICALS shall transfer from Y to X on the completion of the delivery.

Article 6   Payment
Payment from X to Y shall be closed on the last day of each month, and shall be made by issuing promissory notes _____ days after sight.

Article 7   Standards
The standards of CHEMICALS and other technical standards shall be decided upon deliberation [emphasis added].

Article 8   Guarantee

Y shall guarantee that the quality of CHEMICALS conforms to the standards stipulated in the memorandum concluded according to Paragraph 3 of Article 3. Y shall be liable during the term of quality guarantee even after X's receipt of CHEMICALS.

Article 9   Secrecy

Both X and Y shall not divulge to any third party information, know-how and other business secrecy concerning CHEMICALS and its related products obtained through this Contract.

Article 10   Sales of Products Using CHEMICALS

X shall, in principle, sell the products using CHEMICALS. However, Y may sell the products buying them from X at the price to be agreed upon deliberation [emphasis added] between X and Y.

Article 11   Others

Both X and Y are entitled to ask for a reasonable amount of compensation from the other party when one party suffers a loss due to breach of the Contract by the other party.

Article 12   Effective Terms

The Contract shall be valid for 2 (two) years from the date of execution. However, the term shall be extended for another one year on the same conditions if no written objection is issued by either party 3 (three) months before the end of the term. Henceforth the same procedures shall be followed.

Article 13   Deliberation Clause

In case of matters not stipulated in this Contract or if any questions arise regarding the stipulations, X and Y shall decide them upon deliberation [emphasis added].

October ___ , 1983

X: NIPPON LIGHT METAL
COMPANY, LTD.

_____

Y. Matsunaga
President

Y: CHEMICAL COMPANY, LTD.

_____

. . .
President

9 Competitive quality

The affluent Japanese market definitely offers opportunities, but at the same time its affluence sharpens the competition in each industry. Competition is fierce not so much in terms of profit maximization but in terms of the market share domestic competitors want to maintain and expand. Quality is the key, but the competitive quality of the product or service is highly dependent upon the carefully reticulated interdependence of the parties involved. If this interdependence were to be formulated it would look something like: (R&D department and its scientists) *times* (design department and its technicians) *times* (production department and its operators) *times* (purchasing department and its suite of suppliers) *times* (support of QC department) *times* (marketing department and distributors) *times* (the network of retailers and consumers). These variables are seen to interact in a simultaneous way, since the quality of a product or service is believed to be directly related to the quality of the job performed by each and every one involved. Quality is never regarded as a production cost, but as a market requirement.

Furthermore, there are two ways of approaching the marketplace: a company can choose to sell the product or have it bought. When the ultimate aim of a company is to sell the product, it is largely motivated by financial considerations such as profits. New products satisfy the company's need to increase production, and managers hope that the customers will like their products. Attracted by profitability, corporate policy is designed to manipulate the *objective* short-term aspects of marketing, such as costs and price. As a result, the fundamental pricing formula from the marketer's viewpoint would be:

> profits *plus* costs = price

On the other hand, having the product bought is a process that originates and develops in the marketplace (among both customers and competitors). The process is understood in terms of market share. The company focuses on the marketplace to control the *subjective* long-term aspects of marketing, such as the interdependence of suppliers and distributors. In this case, the fundamental pricing formula in reaction to market conditions would be:

> price *minus* costs = profits

In Japan, *to have the product bought* is not only a matter of corporate policy but a law of corporate survival, i.e. in gaining or maintaining market share.

> The single overriding characteristic [of Japanese corporations] is their unrelenting focus on competitive position. They constantly search for growth, driven by the economics of relatively high fixed costs and the dynamics of their system of labor relations. The result is preoccupation with market share and competitive position in contrast to the Western firm's return on investment objective. Leading market share will provide high margins in time, which in turn makes possible investment in still another growth area, and still another drive for leading share. The Western firm's preoccupation with current earnings and current stock price poses no problem when dealing with competitors with the same objectives. A preoccupation with current profits can be a devastating weakness when competing with a market share-preoccupied competitor. That competitor takes a leading share, and in time the profit position reverses. (Abegglen and Stalk 1985: 276)

Japanese firms cannot rely on their products currently sold on the market for survival since they will be emulated by others in no time. Survival is related to growth, not only in the development of the next product but, more importantly, by its acceptance in the market. Hence, quality in the marketplace must be *total*, as expressed by the familiar slogan *Total Quality Control* (TQC), a phrase which is also used in policy-making.

TOTAL QUALITY

Competitive quality secures a kind of 'Holy Alliance' between producers (from boardroom to shopfloor), suppliers, distributors and users. The interdependence of these actors develops into a network based

Table 9.1 Suggestion system, 1980–7

Suggestion system	FY 1980	FY 1985	FY 1987
Number of companies surveyed	427	559	620
Number of employees	1,832,072	1,975,015	2,044,466
Number of suggestions	23,531,908	47,536,255	50,537,412
Rate of participation (per cent)	69.3	60.2	66.6
Rate of adopted suggestions (per cent)	72.0	81.6	86.6
Rate of applied suggestions (per cent)	53.4	72.2	80.5
Corporate benefit from suggestions			
(¥) billion	225.4	346.3	387.7
(Number of companies)	(278)	(350)	(323)
Rewards (¥):			
Total amount (million)	8,179	11,606	11,811
(Number of companies)	(395)	(525)	(565)
Average reward per suggestion	466	387	347
Maximum number of suggestions by one individual	6,919	17,000	14,586

Source: Nihon HR Kyôkai 1988: 8–9

on the expectations shared by them as well as the information contributed by them. The Japanese, whether he is producer or consumer, seller or buyer, looks at a product not as a result of some contracted deal but as the result of participating in a relationship.

Producers

The manufacturer (or, for that matter, the provider of the service) finds it insufficient to be concerned solely with the constant upgrading of the physical aspects of his investment; continuous attention must be given to the upgrading of human resources in terms of technical efficiency as well as marketing competency. The principle at work behind upholding quality is the understanding that quality is not a user's right but a corporate duty. The user's right is initialized at the time of his purchase exchange and quality may then be recognized as just *one* of the factors determining the product's acceptance. Product quality is a corporate duty in every respect, as it is supported by the interdependence of all actors. It is the key ingredient of the product, because it controls the entire process from conception to production to commercialization to consumption. To wit:

Japanese welders (or, as they would be more likely to describe themselves, Japanese company employees who do a lot of welding) take a lot of skill tests. (They have to retake them every three years in fact.) They do so for a variety of reasons – partly for their own personal satisfaction and pride (remember that they live in a society in which there is a great respect for skills), partly, sometimes, in small firms because they would be that much better placed to get a new job if their present firm went bankrupt or they quarrelled with the boss. But usually the overwhelming reason is because their employer wants them to. And he wants them to because of his own quality-consciousness and because he wants orders from quality-conscious customers. (Dore and Sako 1989: 114)

The demand for quality can be seen at the production level, where it is reflected in the eagerness with which Japanese workers provide suggestions. Formulated both on an individual and collective basis, they pour in not because of the reward (less than ¥500 a suggestion on the average) but because of the fact that around 80 per cent of them are implemented (Table 9.1). The average annual rate of suggestions per employee was 4.5 in 1973, rising to 14.7 in 1983, and 24.7 in 1987. Ranked by the total number of suggestions submitted, Matsushita was at the top with 5,038,038 followed by four companies, each with over 2 million. The Ministry of Post and Tele-communications, for long a hotbed of radical unionism, still managed to rank sixteenth, with 543,614 suggestions (Nihon HR Kyôkai 1988: 13 and 35).

The quality in a product is not seen as inherent in the product itself but a feature determined by the corporate system that creates the product. It is not viewed as capital-intensive and thus as an additional cost. Quality is only one aspect in the overall production process. It is an extension of productivity. The responsibility is not assigned to the Quality Control (QC) department nor professionalism of its QC engineers; it is a company-wide responsibility, since corporate performance and corporate image is what is at stake. Operators, for instance, are involved in equipment design, the production process and its scheduling, equipment maintenance, etc. Engineers are on the shopfloor to assist operators, and managers prefer to act more as coordinators than as supervisors. The system generates immediate effects and the reward is a long-term one. 'The development of QC circles must be seen as part of the process in postwar Japan by which the "distribution of intelligence" has been shifted downward to draw on the talents of shop and office floor workers' (Cole 1989: 295).

Japanese manufacturers investing overseas have tried to export their Quality Control experience but the effort is not always greeted with approval, as the reaction of American labour unions has indicated. Thus, the crushing defeat in July 1989 of the United Automobile Workers (UAW) in organizing Nissan's plant in the US made the headlines in Japanese newspapers. Previous to the incident, the UAW had lamely defended its position in its publication, *Solidarity*:

> The key to NUMMI's (GM/Toyota plant in Fremont, California) high productivity is the fully informed worker, not the semi-smart machine.... To develop fully informed workers with a broad range of skills, the UAW agreed to just one job classification for all line workers and just three for the trades. Critics say this historical reversal of protective job demarcation exposes NUMMI workers to the whims of management. But the UAW fought for the more than one hundred job classifications in traditional auto assembly plants precisely because workers had no control over job content on the shop floor. At NUMMI they do. (Quoted in Goldenberg 1988: 173)

The emphasis on quality control is reflected in the way Japanese companies manage their sales force. Sales representatives must report to their offices at the beginning and end of each day to share information with peers and managers and to review moves taken by the competition. The more successful ones help their less talented colleagues in improving their work skills, since rewards will be given according to the group's performance. Contacts with wholesalers and customers are intensely pursued, often by providing all kinds of services, including those which might be considered very personal in nature. At the local level, it is the job of the branch manager to encourage group cohesion and to cultivate an intimate knowledge of market trends and the competition's position among all sales representatives. At the company level, those in senior management are expected to visit all branches regularly and to become well acquainted with top management of important wholesalers and clients.

Suppliers

Suppliers of parts and materials are broadly categorized as general suppliers of standardized products and subcontractors. Subcontractors usually establish the standard for suppliers. Under the fierce competition for market share, new product development is vigorously pursued in respect to the production system (e.g. Just-in-Time) in use, after which the product is standardized and then customized. As the *ideology* of quality control spread, particularly in the 1980s, the common practice of subcontracting changed substantially, in the sense that the unilateral dependence of the subcontractor was increasingly being replaced by mutual interdependence. This change allowed subcontractors to focus on production, since they no longer needed to be involved with selling the product, which stabilized their workload and lessened the risk of doing work that resulted in being unpaid. The parent company's high standards encourage subcontractors to learn from the parent's know-how by receiving its assistance on technical, financial and managerial matters. This kind of guidance fits into the core company's plan to gain the technical skills it lacks and a chance to concentrate on what it does best, to abolish specialized inspection jobs, and to eliminate or reduce the costly discarding of finished or in-process products.

Major companies organize their own associations of subcontractors and suppliers and hold regular monthly meetings to maintain continual close contact with them in order to achieve the high standards of work that will be mutually profitable. In Japanese eyes, such activities are a major source of competitive advantage, at home as well as abroad (Trevor 1988).

Distributors

In comparison to other industrial countries, Japan has extensive distribution routes. The ratio of wholesale to retail sales (value) is more than twice that of other industrial countries with the value added per employee in distribution increasing at a steady rate (Table 9.2). This is largely due to two factors: first, the physical aspects of distribution are severely hampered by the overall shortage of space, creating astronomic land prices, traffic congestion and limited storage space in shops and homes; and, second, financial practices are commonly based on trade credit due to the limited working capital of all but a few retailers. Of the more than 400,000 wholesalers, 75 per cent employ fewer than 10 workers, but among the large wholesalers are giant trading companies such as Mitsui & Co and Mitsubishi Corp. Several layers of wholesalers are needed by the 1.6 million retailers to establish frequent small-lot deliveries, resales being largely transacted on paper with each one including a mark-up. In fact, wholesalers assume much of the risk that is in other countries assumed by retailers themselves. MacKnight observes that

Table 9.2 International comparison of distribution systems

Distribution system		Japan	US	UK	France	FRG
Employment	1975	17.3	20.1	18.0	12.7	13.0
(per cent of total)	1980	17.8	21.1	19.1	13.1	13.3
	1985	17.5	21.9	20.9	13.2	13.1
Value added* (per cent)	1975	55.4	100.0	50.8	81.0	65.1
	1980	71.7	100.0	52.2	86.3	77.9
	1985	72.9	100.0	55.2	83.8	81.4
(Year)		(1982)	(1982)	(1982)	(1983)	(1979)
Number of retail stores per 10,000 population		145.3	82.9	62.7	74.8	67.0
Per cent small retailers		60.2	49.0	–	63.7	–
Ratio of wholesale to retail sales (value)		4.21	1.87	2.03	1.57	1.67
Employees per wholesale store		9.6	12.0	10.8	11.9	10.1

Note:* Value added per head (US = 100, at purchasing power parities).
Source: OECD 1987/8: 80

Small and midsized wholesalers obviously could not take on this pivotal function without the backing of big distributors. They in turn look to particular manufacturers for support, completing the web of dependency that ties the bottom of the distribution chain to the very top and simultaneously puts manufacturers in a position to control the brands stocked by neighborhood retailers and the prices charged. To some analysts this relationship, rather than the complex nature of the distribution system, is what makes it hard for foreign suppliers and domestic newcomers alike to break into the Japanese market. (MacKnight 1989: 7)

Japanese companies deal with the complexity of the system by culti-vating interdependence with their distributors. Long-term relation-ships are established which allow distributors to be a part of the corporate community rather than be treated as outsiders, forming what is known as the distribution *keiretsu*. 'Matsushita Electric Indus-trial Co. has a network of some 28,000 stores around Japan whose loyal owners are considered part of the company's *keiretsu* system and sell Matsushita products at levels close to the maker's recom-mended price. Toshiba's network includes some 15,000 and Hitachi's some 10,000 retailers' (Inoue 1989). Manufacturers rely heavily on distribution channels to *push* the product onto the user. The *keiretsu* requires constant feedback on customer satisfaction. One of the companies that exports its reliance on dealers to the US is Honda Motor.

> Honda is constantly seeking feedback from its dealers. Every U.S. dealer has access to the top marketing executives. Even more important, the dealers feel comfortable calling the executives. All top officers call on dealerships, constantly seeking feedback from 'the people who are closest to the Honda customer.' Honda engineers and manufacturing managers also travel the country to listen to dealers' opinions. They ask the dealers, 'What do you need?' 'What about this?' 'Do you think this will help you sell more cars?' In Japan, every engineering and manufacturing manager, as part of his or her training, is required to spend six months working at a dealership to develop a clear understanding of customer needs. (Shook 1988: 66)

Users

Combining the experience of producers and users is considered normal. One such instance was the successful VLSI project involving semi-conductor firms, Nippon Telephone and Telegraph (NTT), and MITI.

> In the context of the VLSI project, overall development costs were shared. Equipment needs were jointly defined by device and equipment firms, with chip producers using their own prototype wafer fabrication lines as development laboratories for the equipment producers' systems integration and quality improvement efforts. Experiential knowledge built up during the equipment development process thus accrued directly to the *users* of the equipment; the development process typically proceeded under the direction of the very production engineers who would be responsible, ultimately, for implementing the new equipment into production at the chip maker's wafer fab. Not surprisingly, the familiarity of manufacturing engineers with their equipment enabled them to achieve higher yields without constant resort to state-of-the-art technology. Cooperating firms, NTT, and MITI's electrical labs also provided a large, guaranteed internal market that enabled equipment firms to generate learning out of relatively large production runs. (Stowsky 1989: 252–3)

From the Japanese user's viewpoint, quality must be built into the product, supported by the manufacturer, and enhanced by the service that can be provided. After-sales servicing is a responsibility which lies with the manufacturer and is used to obtain the necessary feedback on product performance to stimulate the incentive for further development. Service simply guarantees a product's repeat purchase when total quality is customer-oriented. Komatsu, a leading manufacturer of construction equipment, defines its TQC goal as 'Satisfying Komatsu's worldwide customers through rational, cost-conscious research, development, sales, and servicing' (Imai 1986: 53). It is no wonder that the customer in Japan is not king but *kami-sama* (a god).

MARKETING STRATEGY

Quality is recognized as being more than a mere technical achievement since it stimulates all the objective and subjective faculties of Japanese human resources needed in industry and the marketplace. Work is dedicated to the endless and exciting challenge in achieving quality, to the point where the total economy might be seen as being governed by some industrial and commercial ideology. Companies do not choose between competition or interdependence and instead accept that both exist in a symbiotic relationship. As described in Chapter 8, the business transaction establishes a relationship based on interdependence, as is clearly manifested in Japanese contracts by the emphasis placed on terms such as *upon deliberation*. Competitors must also establish these relationships, causing competition to grow even more intense. This is illustrated by the way household electric appliances are distributed. Their marketing style follows a typical pattern. Manufacturers first promote strong interaction with suppliers, particularly with subcontractors; second, they strive to control channels by the *keiretsu* distribution system; third, some sales entity, often a subsidiary, is established which cushions the brunt of price competition. For example, Hitachi Sales Corp., a Hitachi-controlled wholesaler of household electric appliances, registered a sales-to-profit ratio of 1 per cent in 1989 (Inoue 1989). And, fourth, a centralized marketing department is effectively operated out of headquarters.

The marketing function is centralized in order to face the rapid and continuous changes occurring in an intensely competitive market. The marketing department is usually separated from the sales department, with the former integrated into the head office. 'In Matsushita's case there are strong marketing departments in the head office; each division will sell the products to wholesalers, but it is controlled by the head office. Exporting is operated by an independent subsidiary, Matsushita Trading Company, which has world-wide branches for all Matsushita products' (Kono 1984: 203). Centralization is a significant factor in strengthening marketing operations. Rather than a direct sales force, wholesalers are preferred and they often become the exclusive distribution channels for several corporate divisions. 'In Japan, functional strength and functional integration are more important than integration of the activities for the product or for the geographical area' (*Ibid.*: 301).

Regulating a competition where so much relies on the subjective element has been a challenge to postwar Japan, ever since the US military occupation introduced antimonopoly legislation.

> The Antimonopoly Law gives Japan's Fair Trade Commission authority to take actions against business practices that the FTC deems to be monopolistic.... The mid-1970s were characterized by more violations than either before or after. The number of cases in recent years, however, has fallen to a level far below the average of 34 cases per year between FY 1947 and FY 1972. In FY 1986 and FY 1987 no price-fixing violations by wholesalers were found despite the appreciation of the yen and the likelihood that at least some firms made extraordinary efforts to maintain prices notwithstanding lower yen-denominated costs for their imported products. (Ostrom 1989: 9)

The numerous cartels approved by the FTC are limited to the small/medium firms in local markets, while most trade-conflict cases with the US have been handled under export cartels organized by MITI (JEI 1989a: 12). Mergers, increasing in recent years, are also FTC regulated, and in most cases occur in the small/medium enterprise sector. In Japan, private antitrust suits are rare and their settlement is very modest.

Besides administering the Antimonopoly Law, the Fair Trade Commission also administers the Subcontract Law, which is targeted against large companies that abuse the dominant bargaining positions they hold, and the Premiums and Representations Law which sponsors *Fair Competition Codes*, whereby entrepreneurs or trade associations are allowed, upon FTC authorization, to regulate premiums or representations (over 130 codes have been approved so far). In addition, the FTC provides helpful guidelines relating to various aspects of competition, of which some recent examples are: *Viewpoints on*

Comparative Advertising under the Premiums and Representations Act; Viewpoint on Unreasonable Obstruction of Parallel Imports under Antimonopoly Law; Viewpoints on the Unjust Return of Unsold Goods under the Antimonopoly Law; and *Guidelines for the Regulation of Unfair Trade Practices with Respect to Patent and Know-how Licensing Agreements.* International contracts must be filed with the FTC.

IN FOREIGN FIRMS

The marketing problems of foreign firms in Japan revolve around the *local* image of the foreign product or service. It would be a grave error to expect that the image the foreigner has of his product will be the image that determines his marketing strategy in Japan. The Japanese customer, like any customer anywhere, is primarily influenced by the amount of satisfaction he feels for the product/service. However, this satisfaction is connected to expectation, which is itself affected by the product's image. The foreign product tends to portray itself as *exceptional*, in the sense that it carries the potential of fulfilling needs that the Japanese themselves do not provide for. The product-image can then be described as being created and developed in the following way:

- Initially, the product was not available locally and had to be 'imported-by-ship' (for which the archaic term is *hakurai-hin*, still commonly used in referring to foreign products). New products were indeed imported products for quite some time and so availability was *exceptional*. Hence, questions about their reliability would naturally arise.
- As the product became associated with rapidly growing affluence the higher price was considered reasonable.
- However, consumer expectations would tend to be greater than *normal*, increasing the danger that that product would provide less satisfaction. The normal expectations attached to any given foreign product probably lead to normal expectation in its country of origin, but in Japan, that same level of satisfaction would be *lower* due to higher-than-normal expectations.

The Western firm which believes that Japanese buyers of industrial products or mass retailers are reluctant to buy foreign products just because they are foreign is simply failing to recognize its own shortcomings.

Survey questions concerning purchasing firms' attitudes toward purchasing from foreign sources revealed that roughly two thirds of the firms held positive attitudes. Responses suggested that these attitudes found reflection more in purchasing producer goods than capital goods, but this may simply reflect greater opportunities to import producer goods. Further, when respondents stated attitudes toward purchasing from foreign sources were checked against whether or not they had actually engaged in transactions with such firms, the great majority reported that they had engaged in such transactions. When queried about their prime consideration in making purchases from foreign sources, respondents overwhelmingly noted price and quality for both producer and capital goods. This is in strong contrast to reasons given for maintaining long-term supplier relationships in general. In particular, very few respondents mentioned security of supply or supplier reliability as considerations in choosing foreign suppliers. (FTC 1987: 10)

Success depends on *knowing* the Japanese customer. The case of the pharmaceutical industry described below, with its 180,000 physicians as customers, is only one example which points to the often inadequate effort made in this regard.

For over 30 years a persistent theme has permeated management textbooks – know your customer. Often American firms operating in Japan do not know their customers. Two factors are responsible:
1 The pharmaceutical industry employs approximately 42,000 medical representatives. U.S. firms account for about 12 percent of this total. A few successful companies account for the majority of these employees. There are 180,000 practicing physicians in Japan. Simple arithmetic suggests most U.S. firms directly contact a small percentage of end users through their own sales force.
2 Many U.S. firms have relegated customer contact to Japanese manufacturers through license agreements or joint venture contracts. While this strategy expanded the sales base of innovative products, it left U.S. firms vulnerable to competitive products developed by their Japanese distributors.

This lack of customer contact forces U.S. firms to position their products in the Japanese market based upon experience of user needs in other markets. What is deemed attractive by physicians in the U.S. is assumed to be attractive to Japanese physicians. Successful companies have learned this is not a universal truth. Marketing innovation in Japan, which begins with product development, can only be enhanced by greater knowledge of the Japanese user. (Maurer 1989: 128)

The foreign firm operating in Japan must realize that the determinants of quality as perceived by the home office or the expatriate executive may not be sufficient in meeting local expectations. Competitive quality is determined by both Japanese competitors and Japanese customers. Besides the quality belonging to the product or service itself, additional features are expected because they help local competitors to sell the product. Promotional material must be made available in abundant quantities and in *convincing* Japanese, i.e. not in the form of a mere translation that lacks the power and style to communicate effectively. Furthermore, it must answer questions that Japanese, not foreigners, might ask. All this is presented in colour with sophisticated graphics. Delivery needs to be handled promptly, at the right place, and in the right quantity. Packaging, for a toothbrush or an electric generator, should be done with great care. Defective packaging is reason enough to return the goods to the manufacturer. This applies to the service as well in the sense that it must be *packaged* in the proper greetings and explanations. Great attention is paid to physical appearance and the manner of verbal communication (using *kei-go*, the more polite form of the Japanese language), especially by those dealing directly with the customer; for example, the latter is extremely important in handling queries at the switchboard.

Products and services become recognized as standards in no time but what differentiates them is their corporate image, which in Japan reflects continuity and implies reliability. Customer relations are maintained upon a considerable degree of subjectivity, which makes dealing at arm's length next to impossible. Specifications fitting the client's needs must be pursued to meet his expectations over and above what he obviously needs. The same spirit of cooperation and flexibility is expected from trading intermediaries, who are deeply committed to the transactions they make. In contrast, the Western manufacturer all too often depends on the consumer to *pull* the product through distribution channels.

To consider Japan as a spot market or one that can be handled by remote control from the home office overseas is definitely out of the question. The fierce competition in consumer and industrial markets, the growing technological parity, and the demanding expectations of Japanese customers can only be faced by being in Japan. Establishing and maintaining a competitive position on this market requires a great deal of determination (Chapter 10).

Table 9.3 Marketing the foreign product: entry/exit scenario

Stages	I	II	III	IV	V
Market (units sold)	100	200	400	800	1,600
Foreign: units	100	150	200	250	300
market share	100 per cent	75 per cent	50 per cent	30 per cent	<20 per cent
Local: units	0	50	200	550	1,300
market share	0	25 per cent	50 per cent	70 per cent	>80 per cent
Foreign product					
Image	Foreign	Exceptional but reliable?	Reliable?	'Appropriate'?	Negative?
Price	High	High	Unchanged	Unchanged	Unchanged
Agent's strategy	High margin. 'Pull' advertising	High margin. 'Pull' advertising	High margin. 'Pull' advertising	High margin. Insists on steady performance	High margin. Wants to repeat cycle with new product
Local product					
Image	–	'Me too' (product image)	Available (corporate image)	Adapted (national image)	'Japanized'
Price	–	Somewhat lower	Reduced	Further reduced	'Normal'
Competitor's strategy	–	Own channels. 'Free ride' on foreign advertising	Own channels and 'Push' strategy. 'Free ride'	In-channel promotion (volume)	Broader line of products. Channels abandon foreign product

Entry/exit scenario

For a long time, many new products on the Japanese market were foreign, but as the local competition grew it managed to gain market share that overwhelmed the foreign product. The entry/exit scenario in this context happened all too frequently and provides a valuable lesson on avoiding some present-day pitfalls.

The scenario begins with the principal allowing his product to be handled by a local agent, whose policy is based on securing a product's steady performance to maintain high margins/prices. A *pull* strategy is used, where the product is advertised primarily to users who will pull the product through. This eliminates to a considerable extent sharing margins with distributors. Then faced with the emerging local competition the agent requests that the principal provide a new product to start the cycle all over again. The principal's reaction to the local competition (if he watches market share) is to present a counter-policy suggesting that the agent, first, work harder (e.g. in cultivating distribution channels, tackling local competition), and, second, earn less (reduce margins and lower prices). Both are not very attractive propositions.

On the other hand, high margins on the foreign product attract local competition. The local product takes a free ride on the established foreign image which gives local competitors the necessary time to find the means to *Japanize* the product, progressing even further along the experience curve. Emphasis is placed on a *push* strategy, where the product is carefully promoted to channels in the hope that they will push the product on to the consumer. As the local competition builds up market share, the cultural value of interdependence is brought to bear.

The process can be described in a five-stage scenario, assuming that the market (units sold) doubles at each stage (Table 9.3).

10 Corporate presence and the foreign firm

The foreign firm in postwar Japan evolved from being marginal in the sixties, selective in the seventies, to aggressively competitive in the eighties. Trade and capital liberalization in the sixties and seventies, then import promotion and regional development based on techno-polises (Fujita, Kuniko 1988) in the eighties created greater opportunities. More attention than ever is now given to strengthening corporate presence in Japan as foreign firms operating in Japan today overwhelmingly acknowledge two major incentives for conducting

Table 10.1 Foreign firms: top two major motives for conducting business in Japan by selected industries, 1987 and 1988 (per cent)

Selected industries	Number of firms responding		For growth potential of Japan's markets		To use Japan as a base for Asian business	
	1987	1988	1987	1988	1987	1988
All	1,847	2,295				
	100.0	100.0	42.9	35.0	18.4	26.1
Manufacturing	962	1,166	42.0	33.1	18.2	27.3
Chemicals	213	243	40.4	29.3	19.2	30.5
Pharmaceuticals	57	73	61.4	49.3	7.0	21.9
Oil	24	29	44.4	24.1	33.3	27.6
General machinery	179	223	38.5	30.5	24.0	28.3
Electrical machinery	192	204	37.5	30.4	15.6	26.5
Precision machinery	71	113	42.3	37.2	21.1	26.5
Commerce	656	889	44.2	37.5	18.0	25.1
Services	184	187	41.3	33.7	20.1	24.6

Source: MITI 1989a: 188–9, and 1990c: 162–3

business there: the growth potential of Japan's markets and the ideal position of Japan as a base for doing business in Asia (Table 10.1).

Foreign home offices and their representatives naturally place high expectations on the products or services that they want to offer. Sales turnover is closely watched as a basic indicator of short-term profits or *operations*, but these operations are far from sufficient in achieving success. Their immediate obligations, in whatever legal form, rarely allow executives, either expatriate or at the home office, to prepare themselves adequately for facing the challenge of a Japan that is constantly changing. Furthermore, concentrating on the short-term results of operations could permanently handicap a company's ability in meeting long-term corporate prospects.

This oversight could be compensated by instituting *corporate presence* rather than *operations*, which could then be used to handle the problems of competing in Japan not on the basis of information and experience three, five, or ten years old, but by keeping abreast of the changes occurring in Japan today. As mentioned in Chapter 7, the Japanese show less concern about *acting*, but stress the serious-ness of *re*-acting to reality, since reality is something that is always undergoing change. For them, adapting to these changes is the chal-lenge of survival. To develop human resources in a Japanese way requires adopting such a corporate outlook. But two obstacles stand in the way, one back at the home office, the other in Japan.

THE FOREIGN INVESTOR

Usually the first concern of the foreign investor is maintaining control, which subsequently affects the kind of corporate presence he establishes (Kester 1991). In recent years, many foreign companies have improved their presence, for example by establishing a wholly owned subsidiary or buying out the local partner in a joint venture instead of relying on an agent. Table 10.2 shows some recent exam-ples of changes in market strategy which were noticed in particular companies. One does wonder, however, whether a wholly owned subsidiary has, by itself, a definite advantage over the joint venture. The latter has certainly placed greater focus on operations and is less likely to represent overall corporate interests than the former, but the more fundamental problem of managing and developing the needed human resources, and thus the long-term position on the market, will not be solved simply because there are financial advantages. Referring to American and European joint ventures in Japan, an astute observer concluded that

Table 10.2 Recent changes in market strategy of various companies

Company and type of industry	Former policy	New policy
Giorgio Armani (Italy) Clothing	Agency agreement	Locally established corporation (joint venture)
Herman Miller (US) Furniture	Agency agreement	Locally established corporation (joint venture)
UDG (UK) Whisky	Agency agreement	Sales company (joint venture)
Daimler Benz (Germany) Automobiles	Agency agreement	Locally established sales company (joint venture)
Chrysler (US) Automobiles	Agency agreement	Sales company (joint venture)
Thomas & Betz (US) Electronic parts	Agency agreement	Merger of manufacturing and sales subsidiaries
DEC (US) Computers	Subsidiary	Merger of R&D and sales companies
Siemens (Germany) Electrical machinery	Technology tie-ups	Locally established corporation (joint venture)

Source: JETRO 1989a: 21

The reason for [their] low performance could often be traced to the poor organizational capability of the Western partner to manage and control the cooperative relationship. This deficiency demonstrated itself in a number of firms ranging from ignorance about or misreading of the strategic intentions of their Japanese partner, to disagreements about the implementation of daily business decisions. In particular, the Western firms observed did not pay sufficient attention to the competitive aspects of the joint venture relationship and were not prepared for a possibility of changes in the relative power of their Japanese partners over time. Obviously, more than a single problem factor is generally involved, yet many of these factors share a single characteristic: poorly designed and executed human resource management strategies. In turn, the evidence seems to indicate that many of the problems encountered in designing a human resource strategy for the joint venture are embedded in fundamental differences in the way the two partners approach the human resource role in creating and maintaining competitive advantage. (Pucik 1988: 488)

Many foreign investors perceive joint ventures as a transition to full control. According to one author, in due time 'all joint ventures – even immensely successful ones like Fuji-Xerox, Yokogawa Hewlett-Packard, and Sumitomo 3M – can be expected eventually to break up, be bought out by one of the partners, or go public' (Lacktorin 1989: 36). But another trend may be emerging considering the growing interest in using strategic alliances as a means of globalization, where equity control is not predominant and the quality of human resources is taken as a major issue. In a recent survey, corporate executive officers were asked about the kind of actions they planned to take in the next 12 months to increase their companies' global scope. The forming of new strategic alliances was selected by 44 per cent of the American respondents, 48 per cent of the Europeans, and 60 per cent of the Japanese CEOs (the *Asian Wall Street Journal,* 29 September, 1989: 18).

In the case of Japan, should competitive strategy be mostly the responsibility of the home office or the local representative? Expatriate executives in 31 per cent of the American and 23 per cent of the European firms reported that the corporate management's lack of understanding affected the company's ability to recognize opportunities in Japan, which was a factor in inhibiting greater investment in Japan (Booz, Allen & Hamilton 1987: A–38). The following was observed by two experts in the field of international consulting:

[I]n order to focus corporate attention and resources on the competitive issues and market opportunities that Japan poses, it is often necessary to effect a major organizational change. Japan operations for most companies are a part of a regional organization, or are fragmented among several product organizations. As a result it is difficult to bring to bear the full interest and concerns of the organization in dealing with Japanese issues.... It has proven useful for several major companies to isolate corporate attention on Japan by making Japan operations organizationally separate, which report directly to the chief executive officer. This need not, and organizationally should not, be a permanent reporting pattern. When put in effect for a period of, say, two years, however, it raises the importance of the company's Japan efforts to their appropriate level, forces corporate attention to the issues and opportunities of its Japan position, and helps ensure that sufficient resources of people and capital are available to put an effective strategy for Japan in place. After this is accomplished, the Japan operations can revert to a second-level reporting relationship. (Abegglen and Stalk 1985: 241)

The foreign firm which neglects to recognize Japan on Japanese terms uses financial considerations as a convenient excuse to justify its behaviour. As one survey indicated:

> The time period required to reach corporate average profit levels, compared to alternatives outside of Japan ... was the most frequently cited factor inhibiting greater investment (38 per cent of the respondents). Despite the overall attractive profitability of investments in Japan, there is a strong perception that the start-up time necessary to achieve that level of profitability is longer than other investment alternatives. As a result, Japan does not appear to get the share of a corporation's capital budget or other resources (e.g. people) that might otherwise be devoted to it. There is, however, some evidence that the long timeframe required to reach profitability is more a perceived problem than a real one. On average, it appears to take roughly four years to reach breakeven for a new affiliate in Japan, and seven years to reach corporate average profit levels. Interestingly, these timeframes do not vary considerably between 100 per cent subsidiaries and joint ventures.
> (Booz, Allen & Hamilton 1987: 23)

The lack of understanding at the home office that expatriate executives often complain of is likely due to a preoccupation with results rather than with the process, the reverse of what is taught by Japanese competitors (Chapter 5). *Doing* business may not be much of a problem but the challenge is *staying* in business.

Continuity becomes a necessity, which in Japanese companies is essentially maintained by the *regular* employees, including company-trained managers and executives. By repeating the same process over time, reliability is gradually reinforced. With the relative taboo of acquisitions in Japan, their frequent occurrence in other countries and the rapid turnover of foreign executives often interpreted by the local staff as a clear indication of instability (which in reality may prove to be true), the Japanese market and the Japanese staff cannot help but question the continuity, and thus reliability, of foreign firms.

Competing in Japan demands continuity and patience, as examples brought up earlier have shown. Some salient aspects may be reiterated to stress how important they are.

- Recruiting new high school and college graduates is based on the extent to which direct contacts with schools have been built up over the years; mid-career hiring is only an expedient in fulfilling company goals (Chapter 2). If local competitors are the ones who set the standard, then long-term training and development are expected by the local workforce, i.e. executives, managers and ordinary employees alike. Retaining better employees is indeed a long-term investment (Chapter 3).

- Promotion from within the ranks is still the rule at what are considered reputable companies, though there is evidence of a growing number of exceptions. It is by explicitly acknowledging this rule that the manager at the mid-career level – the exception – should be recruited and retained (Chapter 6). This is difficult in foreign firms, where the turnover of expatriate executives is high, thus creating a situation where long-term objectives of ten years or more are entrusted to a succession of executives serving two- to three-year terms.

- A business contract is not terminated once it has been carried out; in fact, the successful completion of the contract is perceived as one factor behind the ongoing relationship (Chapter 8). In the Japanese market, *one-time* deals rarely occur. Knowledge of, and participation in, long-term subcontracting relationships are essential for doing business in Japan.

Two basic ingredients of *staying* in business in Japan must be brought to the attention of the foreign firm's upper management: the Japanese network of connections and the need for local regrouping.

THE JAPANESE CONNECTION

The old saying 'If you can't beat them, join them', delivers the main message behind gaining access to, and retaining, the kind of human resources foreign firms envy of their Japanese competitors. First of all, *corporate presence* requires that steady contacts be established by getting involved in the numerous instances where Japanese meet each other, get acquainted and talk about business. The lack of concern currently given to Japanese connections is exemplified by the fact that only one out of two foreign firms shows an interest in gaining membership to *any* industrial or trade association in Japan, a situation which showed no signs of improvement even between 1983 and 1987 (MOL 1984: 41 and MOL 1988b: 77). To the local staff, not to mention the public in general, this lack of concern is taken to mean that time and energy spent on participating in the local business world to get acquainted with competitors is considered a waste. Active membership in various trade, industrial and other associations' activities is, of course, time-consuming, but a necessary factor in the overall competition.

(A word of caution: terms such as *trade association, government agency*, and even *bank* must be understood in their Japanese context where, most likely, the foreign businessman may find that his experience gained at home is not adequate to understand the way in which they function, although these institutions may appear to be familiar in some ways. What may be trivial or controversial to the foreigner may look perfectly natural and valid to his Japanese colleagues.)

The foreign firm, i.e. the foreign executives and their Japanese peers and subordinates, must do more than participate actively in their national chamber of commerce in Japan. They must also establish themselves by getting actively involved in the many business organizations to which Japanese competitors belong. Trade associations are known for their effectiveness in circulating information, especially if it comes from abroad, among their members. Much of the interaction between government bureaucracy and business firms takes place in these organizations. They often organize so-called temporary research associations that even qualify for government subsidies. Several foreign companies are members of such prominent organizations as the *Keidanren* (Federation of Economic Organizations) and the *Nikkeiren* (Federation of Employers' Associations), while some expatriate executives belong to the *Keizai Doyukai* (Japan Association of Corporate Executives). Their membership works two ways: the more one contributes, the more one benefits. The amount of time put in by executives (the expatriate and more so his Japanese colleagues) determines the rate of expected returns.

Contrary to what is commonly practised in foreign firms, government relations are not 'used when needed', i.e. sought out at the time a problem arises or upon the visitation of a VIP. Government connections, expertly handled, are needed on a continuous basis. Government-sponsored programmes also include those that accommodate foreign companies and foreign researchers. The Industrial Technology Law (1988) was created to promote international exchange and, under this law, MITI established a new programme of grants-in-aid with eligibility open to foreign companies. The first foreign beneficiary to be named was Dow Chemical of the United States (*Nihon Keizai Shimbun*, 11 April 1989). At the Venice Economic Summit held in 1987, the Japanese government proposed the establishment of a *Human Frontier Science Programme* to bring together international teams for the purpose of conducting basic research on living organisms. The programme was launched in the autumn of 1989 in Strasbourg, France. The participation of foreign corporations has increasingly received greater attention in the planning of Japan's Official Development Assistance (ODA). Domestically, standing relations with local governments are of extreme significance, especially where industrial zones are concerned.

Bank connections, chiefly with the so-called main bank, are not maintained solely on financial terms, for banks supply much valuable information and are reliable sources of business contacts. Domestic banks are vital as partners, often acting as leading shareholders to Japanese firms and providing a sense of security in difficult times (Ballon and Tomita 1988: 60–3). The leading roles these banks now have in the world economy further attests to the solid support they can offer.

The participation of the foreign firm in an industrial grouping (*keiretsu*) is something alien to expatriates and to the home office; hence resentment grows as some restriction is put on freedom of action. But, again, being able to plan the appropriate strategy stems from close cooperation with Japanese counterparts. For local competitors, the *keiretsu* ties stabilize business relationships, help to forward the flow of information among member-companies, and offer planning and financial situations highly appropriate for aggressive long-term corporate growth. Even small firms gain competitive advantage from their participation in the evolving subcontracting system.

The trouble is that many expatriate executives, considering the relatively short period they are posted in Japan, tend to conclude that all these public-relations activities are a waste of time. To their Japanese colleagues, such activities are essential in developing the quality of human resources the foreign firm needs. Being able to adjust to local conditions is a vital part of international business, particularly in the case of Japan.

Patterns of international trade are based not only on exchange rates set by capital markets and legal barriers set by governments but also on the concrete relationships among the firms that actually make buying and selling decisions. To the extent that patterns of industrial organization vary substantially across countries, so too will the purchasing decisions of firms in those countries vary in their sensitivity to economic, social, and political considerations.... Allied firms, quite rationally, base their purchasing decisions on relationships in their entirety rather than on a transaction-specific pricing calculus. As a result of these structural differences in industrial organization, the rules of market access, even among nominally open economies, can have dramatically different results. (Gerlach 1989: 165–6)

Thus, the foreign firm is compelled to take a more comprehensive institutional presence, a presence that can build the human resource potential of the company. Many firms start by local regrouping because the chances are greater that this strategy may facilitate continuity.

LOCAL REGROUPING

Although major foreign multinational corporations in Japan have several subsidiaries and joint ventures they tend to look unrelated, losing the impact that their international size could make where it counts: in the eyes of Japanese customers, distributors, suppliers and employees. Over 90 per cent of the foreign establishments in Japan have less than 300 employees, and 80 per cent less than 100. Furthermore, the company name was thought to be sufficient in establishing themselves locally. But few foreign companies have a corporate *image* in Japan that reflects the kind of reputation that they may have at home. Among the 600 male junior and senior university students surveyed in Tokyo and the Kansai region, the average rate of recognition of 52 major foreign companies was: by name, 19.4 per cent; by name and nationality, 13.8 per cent; by name, nationality and type of industry, 11.1 per cent (Recruit Co. 1984: 7).

In recent years, foreign companies have begun to show a serious interest in regrouping forces locally according to image and expertise, if not also for physical considerations. Thus, many firms have established a sort of Japanese headquarters under one roof (which also saves on the high cost of renting office space). One drawback, though, is that holding companies are illegal in Japan.

[I]t should be noted that Art 9(1) of the [Anti-Monopoly] Law prohibits the establishment of a holding company in Japan. Also, Art 9(2) prohibits foreign companies from operating as holding companies in Japan. The latter would include foreign companies established solely to act as parent companies of joint venture companies in Japan. In order to monitor such shareholdings, the FTC [Fair Trade Commission] requires (i) every non-financial domestic corporation whose total assets exceed two billion yen and (ii) every non-financial foreign corporation to file an annual report of such shareholding with the FTC within three months after the end of each business year. (Oda and Grice 1988: 139–40)

Some centralization in administrative capacity may greatly help operations, not only in filing the annual report but for other reasons as well. The essential basic services that could be centralized are: advertising and public relations in general; legal affairs (intellectual property rights, antimonopoly legislation, contracts on fixed assets, etc.); financial services (banking, accessing financial markets, filing taxes, auditing, etc.); and the participation in various government-subsidized programmes such as research or training, etc.

With local regrouping, a pool of on-the-spot management and technical resources is gradually formed. The time and energy of both the foreign and local personnel can be more effectively utilized under regrouping by centralizing personnel expertise (with the possible exception of personnel administration), especially where different labour unions are active. Having the ability to manufacture or market a foreign product does not automatically qualify an institution and its executives to manage or *develop* their Japanese staff. While directors and managers may be more easily retained when offered ways to expand their careers by dealing with different legal entities, small-size *operations* seem to lack the ability to attract, build up and retain the required human resources.

In addition, local regrouping may encourage a practice common among Japanese competitors called *ama-kudari* (descent from heaven) whereby, coinciding with his retirement, a government official joins a firm in the private sector. This facilitates government relations at crucial times and contributes greatly to the local corporate image. It is also advantageous to select an older Japanese individual (government official, retired ambassador, bank executive, etc.) to occupy a prestigious position, for instance a chairman in the Japanese-style, to have him become the *father figure* for the Japanese workforce (e.g. to help recruit new employees, particularly managers), to have him guide inexperienced expatriates, and so that he can represent the company on public occasions (anniversaries, parties, etc.). Such prestige would have the effect of enhancing presence not merely in the operational sense.

THE ASIAN DIMENSION

The second major reason (in 1987, 18.4 per cent and in 1988, 26.1 per cent of the respondents) why foreign firms decide to establish themselves in Japan is to secure a base for doing business in Asia (see Table 10.1). The global strategy of the home office can be furthered by a sophisticated corporate presence in Japan. The economic advantages of taking such a move are obvious. Between 1978 and 1989, Japan's merchandise trade with Southeast Asia (customs clearance basis) climbed from US$23 billion to US$73 billion in exports, and from US$17 billion to US$53 billion in imports. Japan's cumulative direct investment in Asia amounted to US$40 billion and an increase of $8.2 billion was reported in FY 1989 alone (Keizai Koho Center 1991: 37 and 56).

> Of special significance to corporate planners and national strategists is the fact that, by the turn of the century, Japan is expected to still comprise a full 80 percent of the total East Asia economy – down only very slightly from its present predominant position. Any strategy for Asia, then, must be based on a strategy for Japan, which will continue as the source of capital, technology and aid for the area, and will be the major market for the area's products.
> (Abegglen 1989)

Countries in East Asia are determined to repeat what Japan's economic performance has demonstrated in the last 40 years: first, catching up with the Western developed world and, second, doing so despite, or due to, non-Western roots. This has acted as a catalyst in the Asian development strategy as is visible in Singapore's 'Learn from Japan' or Malaysia's 'Look East' slogans for promoting growth. The social, economic and political changes that East Asia has undergone in the last two decades point to the end of an era where the West dominated world affairs for two or more centuries. For the Western executive, active on a global scale, it means adjusting to a business environment that is slowly becoming non-Westernized. The nineteenth-century mentality – the West as hegemony – is hard to undo. But as Asia, led by Japan, is increasingly in a position to teach some new lessons, the Westerner must take a second look at himself. Policies, systems and operational methods in business and other fields readily considered as sacred back home, will then be exposed for their positive and/or negative worth.

This re-evaluation suggests that there are some differences in the quality of human resources. Asian human resources, as exemplified by Japan, have some characteristics that set them apart from familiar Western behaviour. (Some analysts have even attempted to uncover the common human factor among East Asian countries by attributing it to the Confucian tradition.) The challenge is not in developing human resources that are *Japanese*-like but in applying plain common sense, a commodity of which neither the Westerner nor the Japanese has a monopoly. It is not the product or the price that determines competitive strength, but the people who make, sell, and use that product. A different environment with contending social and economic aspects emerges. This is a dimension of industrial and corporate policy that upsets most generally accepted theories and practices (Johnson 1988). In Japan, the economic environment has been visualized less in terms of material resources and more in terms of human resources. Asian economies pursue non-Western qualities of development strategy in realizing their own potential. Their goal is not to imitate the Japanese but to emulate them. In the nineteenth century and throughout most of the twentieth century, Japan was recognized in the West as 'the first non-Western nation to *industrialize*' – to become more like the West. Towards the end of the twentieth century East Asia managed to shift the emphasis to *non-Western*, where Japan is now declared to be 'the first *non-*Western nation to industrialize' and is to be emulated in these terms.

Bibliography

Abegglen, James C. (1984) *The Strategy of Japanese Business*, Cambridge, Massachusetts: Ballinger.
—— (1989) 'The Fast Pace of Asian Change' *Venture Japan*, vol. 1, no. 4, p. 7.
Abegglen, James C. and Stalk, George, Jr. (1985) *Kaisha, the Japanese Corporation*, New York: Basic Books.
ACCJ (American Chamber of Commerce in Japan), Tokyo (1979) *United States' Manufacturing Investment in Japan*, July.
—— (1988) *Gaishi-kei Kigyô Rikuruto Gaido* [Foreign Firms' Recruit Guide].
Amaya, Tadashi (1983) *Human Resource Development in Industry*, Tokyo: Japan Institute of Labour.
—— (1990) *Recent Trends in Human Resource Development*, Tokyo: Japan Institute of Labour.
Aoki, Masahiko (1988) *Information, Incentives, and Bargaining in the Japanese Economy*, Cambridge: Cambridge University Press.
Balassa, Bela and Noland, Marcus (1988) *Japan in the World Economy*, Washington, DC: Institute for International Economics.
Ballon, Robert J. (1988) *Business Contracts in Japan*, Tokyo: Sophia University Institute of Comparative Culture, Business Series, no. 122.
—— (1989) *The Subcontracting System: Challenge to Foreign Firms*, Tokyo: Sophia University Institute of Comparative Culture, Business Series, no. 127.
—— (1990a) *Decision Making in Japanese Industry*, Tokyo: Sophia University Institute of Comparative Culture, Business Series, no. 132.
—— (1990b) *The Salary System and Foreign Firms*, Sophia University Institute of Comparative Culture, Business Series, no. 133.
Ballon, Robert J. and Tomita, Iwao (1988) *The Financial Behavior of Japanese Corporations*, Tokyo: Kodansha International.
Batzer, Erich and Laumer, Helmut (1989) *Marketing Strategies and Distribution Channels for Foreign Companies in Japan*, Boulder: Westview.
Booz, Allen & Hamilton, Inc. (1987) *Direct Investment in Japan: The Challenge for Foreign Firms. A Study for the ACCJ (American Chamber of Commerce in Japan) and EBS (Council of the European Business Community)*, Tokyo, September.
Calder, Kent E. (1988) *Crisis and Compensation. Public Policy and Political Stability in Japan, 1949–1986*, Princeton: Princeton University Press.

Chalmers, Norma J. (1989) *Industrial Relations in Japan. The Peripheral Workforce*, London: Routledge.

CLRC (Central Labour Relations Commission), Tokyo (1989a) *Taishoku-kin, Teinen-sei oyobi Nenkin Jijô Chôsa* [Survey on Separation Allowance, Age-limit and Old-age Pension], June.

—— (1989b) *Chingin Jijô Chôsa* [Survey of Wages].

Cole, Robert E. (1989) *Strategies for Learning. Small-Group Actitivies in American, Japanese, and Swedish Industry*, Berkeley: University of California Press.

Contractor, Frank J. and Lorange, Peter (eds) (1988) *Cooperative Strategies in International Business*, Lexington: Lexington Books.

Dore, Ronald (1983) 'Goodwill and the Spirit of Market Capitalism', *The British Journal of Sociology*, vol. 34, no. 4, pp. 439–81.

Dore, Ronald P. and Sako, Mari (1989) *How the Japanese Learn to Work*, London: Routledge.

Eccleston, Bernard (1989) *State and Society in Post-War Japan*, Cambridge: Polity Press.

EPA (Economic Planning Agency), Tokyo (1988) *Economic Survey of Japan, 1987–1988*.

—— (1990) *Economic Survey of Japan, 1988–1989*.

Ernst, Angelika and Laumer, Helmut (1989) *Struktur und Dynamik der mittelstandischen Wirtshaft in Japan*, Hamburg: Mitteilungen des Instituts für Asienkunde, Nr. 170.

Fields, George (1983) *From Bonsai to Levi's. When West Meets East: An Insider's Surprising Account on How the Japanese Live*, New York: Macmillan.

—— (1988) *The Japanese Market Culture*, Tokyo: The Japan Times.

Finn, Richard B. (ed.) (1986) *US–Japan Relations: Learning from Competition. Annual Review*, 1985, New Brunswick (US): Transaction Books.

FTC (Fair Trade Commission), Tokyo (1983) *Sôgô Shôsha no Jigyô Katsudô no Jittai Chôsa* [Survey of the Activities of General Trading Companies], April.

—— (1987) *Long-Term Relationships Among Japanese Companies. A Report by the Study Group on Trade Frictions and Market Structure*, April (mimeographed).

Fujita, Kuniko (1988) 'The Technopolis: High Technology and Regional Development in Japan', *International Journal of Urban and Regional Research*, vol. 12, no. 4 (December), pp 566–94.

Fujita, Yoshitaka (1984) *Employee Benefits and Industrial Relations*, Tokyo: Japan Institute of Labour.

Gerlach, Michael (1989) '*Keiretsu* Organization in the Japanese Economy. Analysis and Trade Implications', in Johnson *et al.* 1989, pp 141–74.

Glazer, Herbert (1987) *Japanese High Technology. Questions and Answers*, Tokyo: Sophia University Institute of Comparative Culture, Business Series, no. 114.

—— (1991) *Corporate Research Laboratories in Japan*, Tokyo: Sophia University Institute of Comparative Culture, Business Series, no. 134.

Goldenberg, Susan (1988) *Hands Across the Ocean. Managing Joint Ventures with a Spotlight on China and Japan*, Boston: Harvard Business School Press.

Graham, John L. (1988) 'Deference Given the Buyer: Variations across Twelve Cultures', in Contractor and Lorange 1988, pp 473–85.

Graves, Stephen (1989) *Corporate Flexibility in Japan*, Tokyo: Sophia University Institute of Comparative Culture, Business Series, no. 126.

Green, Gretchen (1989) *Education in Japan*, Report no. 7A (February 17), Washington, DC: Japan Economic Institute (mimeographed).

Gregory, Gene (1982) *The Logic of Japanese Enterprise*, Sophia University Institute of Comparative Culture, Business Series, no. 92.

—— (1986) *Japanese Electronics Technology: Enterprise and Innovation. (Second Edition)* Tokyo: The Japan Times.

Grice, R. Geoffrey (1988) 'Joint Ventures with Japanese Companies – Problems of Anti-Monopoly Law', in Oda and Grice 1988, pp. 129–43.

Haley, John O. (1982) 'Sheating the Sword of Justice in Japan: An Essay on Law Without Sanctions', *The Journal of Japanese Studies*, vol. 8, no. 2 (Summer), pp 265–81.

Hanami, Tadashi (1979) *Labour Relations in Japan Today*, Tokyo: Kodansha International.

—— (1983) 'Unfair Labor Practices: Law and Practice', *Japan Labour Bulletin*, vol. 22, no. 6 (June), pp 5–8.

Hattori, Ichiro (1978) 'A Proposition on Efficient Decision-Making in the Japanese Corporation', *Columbia Journal of World Business*, Summer, pp 7–15.

Hayashi, Kichiro (1978) 'Corporate Planning Practices in Japanese Multinationals', *Academy of Management Journal*, vol. 21, no. 2, pp 211–26.

Hayashi, Kichiro (ed.) (1989) *The U.S.–Japanese Economic Relationship: Can it Be Improved?* New York: New York University Press.

Hayashi, Shuji (1988) *Culture and Management in Japan*, Tokyo: Tokyo University Press.

Henderson, Dan Fenno (1973) *Foreign Enterprise in Japan. Laws and Policies.* Chapel Hill: University of North Carolina Press.

Hirose, Katsusada (1989) 'Corporate Thinking in Japan and in the U.S.', *Journal of Japanese Trade and Industry*, vol. 8, no. 4, pp 40–3.

Huddleston, Jackson N., Jr. (1990) *Gaijin Kaisha. Running A Foreign Business in Japan*, Armonk, NY: Sharpe.

IIBC (Institute for International Business Communication), Tokyo (1987) *Foreign Affiliates in Japan: The Search for Professional Manpower.*

Imai, Masaaki (1986) *Kaizen. The Key to Japan's Competitive Success.* New York: Random House.

IMD Journal, Brussels (1989) 'The Japanese Learning Organization', no. 4.

Inagami, Takeshi (1981) 'The Japanese Will to Work', *The Wheel Extended*, vol. 10, no. 3 (January–March), pp 21–9.

—— (1988) *Japanese Workplace Industrial Relations*, Tokyo: Japan Institute of Labour.

Inohara, Hideo (1990a) *Personnel Appraisal in Japanese Companies*, Tokyo: Sophia University Institute of Comparative Culture, Business Series, no. 128.

—— (1990b) *The Japanese Personnel Department: Structure and Functions*, Tokyo: Sophia University Institute of Comparative Culture, Business Series, no. 132.

—— (1990c) *Human Resource Development in Japanese Companies*, Tokyo: Asian Productivity Organization.

Inoue, Yuko (1989) 'Manufacturers at War with Discount Retailers', *The Japan Economic Journal,* 19 August, 1989, p. 32.

Ishizumi, Kanji (1988) *Acquiring Japanese Companies. A Guidebook for Entering the Japanese Market through M&A,* Tokyo: The Japan Times.

Iwata, Ryushi (1982) *Japanese-Style Management: Its Foundations and Prospects,* Tokyo: Asian Productivity Organization.

JEI (Japan Economic Institute), Washington, DC (1989a) *Japan's Competition Policies,* no. 20A, 19 May.

—— (1989b) *Statistical Profile: Japan's Economy in 1988 and International Transactions of Japan and the United States in 1988,* no. 39A, 13 October.

JETRO (Japan External Trade Organization), Tokyo (1982) *Foreign Companies in Japan.*

—— (1989a) *1989 JETRO White Paper on World Direct Investments. Summary.*

—— (1989b) *NIPPON 1989. Business Facts and Figures.*

—— (1990) *NIPPON 1990. Business Facts and Figures.*

JIL (Japan Institute of Labour), Tokyo (1989) *Japanese Working Life Profile. Statistical Aspects.*

—— (1990) *Japan Labour Bulletin.* vol. 29, no. 4 (April).

Johnson, Chalmers (1982) *MITI and the Japanese Miracle. The Growth of Industrial Policy, 1925–1975,* Stanford: Stanford University Press.

—— (1988) 'The Japanese Political Economy: A Crisis in Theory', *Ethics & International Affairs,* vol. 2, pp 79–97.

Johnson, Chalmers, Tyson, Laura D'Andrea, and Zysman, John (eds) (1989) *Politics and Productivity. How Japan's Development Strategy Works,* New York: Ballinger.

JPC (Japan Productivity Center), Tokyo (1982) *Indices 1982.*

Kagono, Tadao; Nonaka, Ikujiro; Sakakibara, Kiyonori; Okumura, Akihiro (1985) *Strategic vs. Evolutionary Management. A U.S.–Japan Comparison of Strategy and Organization,* Amsterdam: North-Holland.

Kang, T.W. (1990) *Gaishi. The Foreign Company in Japan,* New York: Basic Books.

Keizai Koho Center, Tokyo (1991) *Japan 1991. An International Comparison.*

Kester, W. Carl (1991) *Japanese Takeovers. The Global Contest for Corporate Control,* Boston: Harvard Business School Press.

Kikuchi, Makoto (1981) 'Creativity and Ways of Thinking: the Japanese Style', *Physics Today,* September, pp 42–51.

Koh, B.C. (1989) *Japan's Administrative Elite,* Berkeley: University of California Press.

Koike, Kazuo (1983) 'Workers in Small Firms and Women in Industry', in Shirai 1983, pp 89–115.

—— (1987) 'Human Resource Development and Labor-Management Relations', in Yamamura and Yasuba 1987, pp 289–330.

—— (1988) *Understanding Industrial Relations in Modern Japan,* London: Macmillan.

Komai, Hiroshi (1989) *Japanese Management Overseas. Experiences in the United States and Thailand,* Tokyo: Asian Productivity Organization.

Komiya, Ryutaro; Okuno, Masahiro; Suzumura, Kotaro (eds) (1988) *Industrial Policy of Japan,* Tokyo: Academic Press.

Kono, Toyohiro (1984) *Strategy & Structure of Japanese Enterprises,* London: Macmillan.

Lacktorin, Michael J. (1989) *Foreign Direct Investment in Japan. The Long-term Strategy for the Japanese Market,* Tokyo: Sophia University Institute of Comparative Culture, Business Series, no. 125.

Lincoln, James R. and Kalleberg, Arne L. (1990) *Culture, Control, and Commitment. A Study of Work Organization and Work Attitudes in the United States and Japan,* Cambridge: Cambridge University Press.

Lynn, Leonard H. and McKeown, Timothy J. (1988) *Organizing Business. Trade Associations in America and Japan,* Washington, DC: American Enterprise Institute for Public Policy Research.

MacKnight, Susan (1989) 'Japan's Distribution System: The Next Major Trade Confrontation?' *JEI Report,* no. 11A (17 March). Washington, DC.

Makino, Shojiro (1987) 'Relationship with Customers and Suppliers', Tokyo: Sophia University (mimeographed).

Matsumoto, Michihiro (1984) *Haragei,* Tokyo: Kodansha.

Matsushita, Mitsuo and Schoenbaum, Thomas J. (1989) *Japanese International Trade and Investment Law,* Tokyo: University of Tokyo Press.

Maurer, P. Reed (1989) 'Competing in Japan', Tokyo: *The Japan Times.*

McCormack, Gavan and Sugimoto, Yoshio (eds) (1986) *Democracy in Contemporary Japan,* Sydney: Hale & Hyremonger.

Minato, Tetsuo (1989) 'A Comparison of Japanese and American Interfirm Production Systems', in Hayashi, Kichiro (ed.) 1989, pp 87–122.

MITI (Ministry of International Trade and Industry), Tokyo (1976) *White Paper on Small and Medium Enterprises in Japan 1976.*

—— (1986) *White Paper on Small and Medium Enterprises in Japan 1986.*

—— (1987a) *Gaishi-kei Kigyô no Dôkô, Dai 19 Kai* [The Situation of Foreign Capital Affiliated Firms, 19th Survey].

—— (1987b) *Shôwa 62-nen Ban. Sôgô Keiei-ryoku Shihyô, Seizô-gyô* [Index of Overall Management Ability, 1987 – Manufacturing Industry].

—— (1987c) *Shôwa 62-nen Ban. Sôgô Keiei-ryoku Shihyô, Ko-uri-gyô Hen* [Index of Overall Management Ability, 1987 – Retail Industry].

—— (1989a) *Gaishi-kei Kigyô no Dôkô, Dai 20-21 Kai* [The Situation of Foreign Capital Affiliated Firms, 20th–21st Survey].

—— (1989b) Press release, May.

—— (1989c) *News from MITI. NR-366 (89-9).* July.

—— (1989d) *Heisei Gan-nen. Sôgô Keiei-ryoku Shihyô, Seizô-gyô* [Index of Overall Management Ability, 1989 – Manufacturing Industry].

—— (1989e) *Heisei Gan-nen. Sôgô Keiei-ryoku Shihyô, Ko-uri-gyô Hen* [Index of Overall Management Ability, 1989 – Retail Industry].

—— (1990a) *News from MITI. NR-374 (90-3),* January.

—— (1990b) *News from MITI. NR-377 (90-6),* March.

—— (1990c) *Gaishi-kei Kigyô no Dôkô, Dai 22-23 Kai* [The Situation of Foreign Capital Affiliated Firms, 22nd–23rd Survey].

—— (1990d) *White Paper on Small and Medium Enterprises in Japan 1990.*

Mito, Setsuo (1981) *Honda Manajimento Shistemu* [Honda Management System], Tokyo: Diamondo-sha.

Miyai, J. (1985) *On Being a Japanese Manager in a Foreign Firm,* Tokyo: Sophia University Institute of Comparative Culture, Business Series no. 103.

MOE (Ministry of Education), Tokyo (1988) *Basic Survey of Schools 1988*.
MOL (Ministry of Labour), Tokyo (1973) *Rôdô Haku-sho* [White Paper on Labour].
—— (1985) *Shôwa 60-nenban Nihon no Rôshi Communication no Genjo* [Actual Situation of Labour-management Communications in Japan, 1985].
—— (1987a) *Shôwa 62-nen Koyô Kanri Chôsa* [Survey on Employment and Personnel Management, 1987].
—— (1987b) *Rôdô Kumiai Kihon Chôsa* [Basic Survey of Labour Unions].
—— (1988a) *Year Book of Labor Statistics, 1987*, December.
—— (1988b) *Gaishi-kei Kigyô no Rô-shi Kankei no Jittai Chôsa Hôkoku-sho* [Survey Report on the Actual Situation of Labour–Management Relations in Foreign Capital Affiliated Enterprises], May.
—— (1988c) *Maigetsu Kinrô Tôkei Chôsa Nempô* [Annual Report on the Monthly Labour Statistical Survey].
—— (1988d) *Rôdô Haku-sho* [White Paper on Labour].
—— (1988e) *Chingin Kôzô Kihon Chôsa Hôkoku* [Report on the Basic Survey of Wage Structure], vol. 3.
—— (1988f) *Maigetsu Kinrô Tôkei Chôsa Geppô* [Monthly Bulletin on the Labour Statistics Survey], no. 475 (August).
—— (1988g) *Shôwa 62-nen Chingin Kôzô Kihon Chôsa Hôkoku* [Report on the Basic Statistical Survey of Wage Structure 1987], vol. 1.
—— (1988h) *Labour Issues Quarterly*, no. 1 (Autumn).
—— (1989a) *Maigetsu Kinrô Tôkei Chôsa Geppô* [Monthly Bulletin on the Labour Statistics Survey], no. 480 (January).
—— (1989b) Press Release, May.
—— (1989c) *Chingin Kôzô Kihon Chôsa* [Basic Survey of Wage Structure].
—— (1989d) *Maigetsu Kinrô Tôkei Chôsa Geppô* [Monthly Bulletin on the Labour Statistics Survey], no. 487 (August).
—— (1989e) *Rôdô Kumiai Kihon Chôsa Hôkoku* [Report on the Basic Survey of Labour Unions].
—— (1989f) *Rôdô Sôgi Tôkei Chôsa Nen-hôkoku* [Annual Report on the Statistical Survey of Labour Disputes].
—— (1989g) *Chingin Kôzô Kihon Tôkei Chôsa Hôkoku* [Report on the Basic Statistical Survey on Wage Structure], vol. 3.
—— (1989h) *Year Book of Labour Statistics, 1988*
—— (1989i) *Rôdô Haku-sho* [White Paper on Labour].
—— (1990a) *Rôdô Kumiai Kihon Chôsa Hôkoku* [Report on the Basic Survey of Labour Unions].
—— (1990b) *Rôdô Haku-sho* [White Paper on Labour].
Monden, Yasuhiro (1983) *Toyota Production System*, Atlanta: Industrial Engineering and Management Press.
Moritani, Masanori (1982) *Japanese Technology*, Tokyo: Simul.
Mouer, Ross and Sugimoto, Yoshio (1989) 'A Multi-dimensional View of Stratification: A Framework for Comparative Analysis', in Sugimoto and Mouer 1989, pp 157–201.
Murakami, Kiyoshi (1988) *Retirement Benefits and Pension Plans in Japan*, Tokyo: Sophia University Institute of Comparative Culture, Business Series, no. 118.
Nakagawa, M. (1988) 'Trade Friction and the Anti-Monopoly Legislation of

Japan – Activities of the Fair Trade Commission', in Oda and Grice 1988, pp 144–56.

Nakatani, Iwao (1988) *The Japanese Firm in Transition*, Tokyo: Asian Productivity Organization.

National Land Agency, Tokyo (1987) *The Fourth Comprehensive National Development Plan*, June.

National Tax Administration, Tokyo (1990) *Shôwa 63-nenbun Zeimu-tôkei kara Mita Hôjin Kigyô no Jittai* [Actual Situation of Juridical-Entity Enterprises from the Viewpoint of Taxation Statistics, 1988].

NIEVR (National Institute for Employment and Vocational Research), Tokyo (1987) *Kigyô-group-nai Jinzai Katsuyo ni Kansuru Chôsa Kenkyû Hôkokusho* [Report on the Survey on Human Resource Utilization in Enterprise Groups].

Nihon HR (Human Relations) Kyôkai, Tokyo (1988) *Sôi to Kufû* [Creativity and Technique], no. 92 (September).

Nikkei Business, Tokyo (1989) *Yoi Kaisha. Chôju Kigyô no Jôken* [Good Companies. Conditions in Long-life Enterprises].

Nikkeiren (Japan Federation of Employers' Associations), Tokyo (1981) *Report of the Committee for the Study of Labour Questions*. March.

—— (1990a) *Report of the Committee for the Study of Labour Questions*.

—— (1990b) *Shôkyû Besu-appu Jisshi Jôkyô Chôsa Kekka* [Results of the Survey on Salary Increase and Base-up], November.

Nonaka, I. and Okumura, A. (1984) 'Comparison of Management in American, Japanese and European Firms (I)', *Management in Japan*, 17, no. 1 (Spring), pp 23–40.

NPA (National Personnel Authority), Tokyo (1987) *Kyûyo Jitsumu Yôran* [Handbook of Pay Practices].

—— (1989a) *Minkan Kyûyo no Jittai* [Actual Earnings in the Private Sector].

—— (1989b) *Jinji-In Geppô* [National Personnel Authority Monthly News], September.

—— (1990) *Minkan Kyûyo no Jittai* [Actual Earnings in the Private Sector].

Oda, Hiroshi and Grice, R. Geoffrey (eds) (1988) *Japanese Banking, Securities and Anti-Monopoly Law*, London: Butterworths.

OECD (Organization for Economic Cooperation and Development), Paris (1986) *Economic Surveys: Japan*.

—— (1987/88) *Economic Surveys: Japan*.

—— (1989) *OECD in Figures. Statistics on the Member Countries 1989*.

Ohmae, Kenichi (1989) 'The Global Logic of Strategic Alliances', *Harvard Business Review*, March–April, pp 143–54.

Ohta, Toshiaki (1988) 'Work Rules in Japan', *International Labour Review*, vol. 127 (1988), no. 5, pp 627–39.

Okimoto, Daniel I. and Rohlen, Thomas P. (eds) (1988) *Inside the Japanese System*, Stanford: Stanford University Press.

Osawa, Machiko (1989) 'The Service Economy and Industrial Relations in Small and Medium Size Firms in Japan', *Japan Labor Bulletin*, vol. 28, no. 7 (July), pp 4–8.

Ostrom, Douglas (1989) *Japan's Competition Policies*, Report no. 20A (19 May). Washington, DC: Japan Economic Institute (mimeographed).

Pucik, Vladimir (1988) 'Strategic Alliances with the Japanese: Implications for Human Resource Management', in Contractor and Lorange 1988: 487–98.

Ramseyer, J. Mark (1986) 'Lawyers, Foreign Lawyers, and Lawyers Substitutes: The Market for Regulation in Japan', *Harvard International Law Journal*, vol. 27, special issue.

Recruit Co. Tokyo (1984) *Survey on University Students' Preference and Image of Foreign Companies.*

Rohlen, Thomas P. (1988) 'Education in Japanese Society', in Okimoto and Rohlen (1988), pp 25–31.

Samuels, Richard J. (1987) *The Business of the Japanese State. Energy Markets in Comparative and Historical Perspective*, Ithaca: Cornell University Press.

Saso, Mary (1990) *Women in the Japanese Workplace*, London: Shipman.

Sawada, J. Yoshio (1968) *Subsequent Conduct and Supervening Events*, Tokyo: University of Tokyo Press.

Schmiegelow, Michele (1986) *Japan's Response to Crisis and Change in the World Economy*, Armonk, NY: Sharpe.

Seikei Kenkyusho, Tokyo (1988) *'89 Nendo-ban Yaku-in no Hôshû, Shôyo, Nenshû* [Remuneration, Bonus, Annual Income of Executives, FY1989].

Sekiguchi, Sueo (1986) 'Industrial Policy in Japan: Interaction between Policies and Dualist Structure', in Schmiegelow 1986: 230–56.

Shimizu, Ryûei (1989) *The Japanese Business. Success Factors*, Tokyo: Chikura Shobo.

Shinotsuka, Eiko (1989) 'Japanese Women's Limited Job Choices', *Economic Eye*, vol. 10, no. 1 (Spring), pp 27–30.

Shirai, Taishiro (ed.) (1983) *Contemporary Industrial Relations in Japan*, Madison: University of Wisconsin Press.

Shook, Robert L. (1988) *Honda. An American Success Story*, New York: Prentice Hall.

Sone, Yasunori (1989) 'Interest Groups and the Process of Political Decision-making in Japan', in Sugimoto and Mouer 1989, pp 259–95.

Statistics Bureau, Tokyo (1990) *Japan Statistical Yearbook 1990*, November.

Stowsky, Jay S. (1989) 'Weak Links, Strong Bonds. U.S.–Japanese Competition in Semiconductor Production Equipment', in Johnson *et al.* 1989, pp 241–74.

Sugeno, Kazuo (1989) 'Shukko (Transfers to Related Firms): An Aspect of the Changing Labor Market in Japan', *Japan Labour Bulletin*, vol. 28, no. 4 (April), pp 3–8.

Sugimoto, Yoshio and Mouer, Ross E. (eds) (1989) *Constructs for Understanding Japan*, London: Kegan Paul.

Taira, Koji (1983) 'Japan's Low Unemployment: Economic Miracle or Statistical Artifact?' *Monthly Labour Review*, July, pp 3–10.

Takanashi, Akira *et al.* (1989) *Shunto Wage Offensive. Historical Overview and Prospects*, Tokyo: Japan Institute of Labour.

Takashina, Shûji (1988) 'Probing Japan's Consensus Society', *Japan Echo*, vol. XV, no. 2 (Summer), pp 50–1.

Tanaka, Hideo (1976) *The Japanese Legal System: Introductory Cases and Materials*, Tokyo: Tokyo University Press.

Tokunaga, Shigeyoshi (1983) 'A Marxist Interpretation of Japanese Industrial

Relations, with Special Reference to Large Private Enterprises', in Shirai 1983, pp 313–29.

Tokyo Municipal Government, Labour Department, Tokyo (1988) *Chûsho Kigyô no Chingin Taishoku-kin Jijô* [Situation of Wages and Separation Allowance in Small-medium Enterprises], December.

Trevor, Malcolm (1988) *Toshiba's New British Company. Competitiveness through Innovation in Industry*, London: Policy Studies Institute.

Trevor, Malcolm and Christie, Ian (1988) *Manufacturers and Suppliers in Britain and Japan*, London: Policy Studies Institute.

TSE (Tokyo Stock Exchange), Tokyo (1990) *Fact Book 1990*.

Umetani, Shunichiro (1980) *Vocational Training in Japan*, Hamburg: Institut für Asienkunde, no. 114.

Wagatsuma, Hiroshi and Rosett, Arthur (1986) 'The Implications of Apology: Law and Culture in Japan and the United States', *Law and Society Review*, vol. 20, no. 4, pp 461–98.

Watanabe, Takehiko and Mochizuki, Hiroshi (1986) 'Perception Gap Between the U.S. and Japan: Delegation and Sharing of Authority and Responsibility', in Finn 1986, pp 85–100.

Wheeler, Jimmy W.; Janow, Merit E.; Pepper, Thomas (1982) *Japanese Industrial Development Policies in the 1980s. Implications for U.S. Trade and Investment*, Croton-on-Hudson: Hudson Institute, October.

Whitehill, Arthur M. (1991) *Japanese Management. Tradition and Transition*, London: Routledge.

Yamamoto, Shichibei (1984) *Nemawashi no Shisô* [The Philosophy of Nemawashi], Tokyo: Gakken.

Yamamura, Kozo and Yasuba, Yasukichi (eds) (1987) *The Political Economy of Japan. Volume 1 – The Domestic Transformation*. Stanford: Stanford University Press.

Yokokura, Takashi (1988) 'Small and Medium Enterprises', in Komiya *et al.* 1988, pp 513–39.

Yoshida, Junichi (1989) *Produktinnovation in Japan. Ein Weg zum ganzheitlichen Produktmarketing*, Vienna: Service.

Yuzawa, Takeshi and Udagawa, Masaru (eds) (1990) *Foreign Business in Japan Before World War II*, Tokyo: University of Tokyo Press.

Glossary

Ama-kudari: 'descent from heaven,' speaking of the high government official who upon retirement joins a company in the private sector
Arasoi wo mizu ni nagasu: 'let the dispute flow with the water'

Bu-chô: department head
Bunsho-ka: archive section (at corporate headquarters)

Chôsei teate: adjustment allowance
Chûto saiyô: mid-career hiring

Daihyô torishimari-yaku: representative director
Daini kuimiai: second (rival) labour union in the same enterprise
Dairi: assistant to (a manager)
Dantai kôshô: collective bargaining (with labour union)
Dantai kyôyaku: collective labour agreement (with labour union)

Fuku: deputy (manager)
Fuku sha-chô: executive vice president
Fuyô teate: dependants' allowance

Gekkyû: monthly earnings
Genryô keiei: 'trimming-fat management' for corporate rationalization
Gôhô: rank (in government basic salary tables)
Gyôsei shidô: administrative guidance

Habatsu: clique
Hakurai-hin: goods imported by ship; imported goods
Hanchô: foreman

Hôki-ka: legal section (at corporate headquarters)
Hômu-ka: legal section (at corporate headquarters)
Honbu-chô: division head
Honpô: basic salary
Hon-sha: corporate headquarters
Hosa: assistant to (a manager)

Ippan sha-in: rank-and-file employees

Ji-chô: intermediate position between *ka-chô* and *buchô*
Jiko-tsugô: private initiative, stands for voluntary separation
Jinji-bu: personnel department
Jinji-in: National Personnel Authority
Jinji-ka: personnel section
Jirei: notice
Jôhô shakai: information society
Jômu: managing director
Jômu-kai: executive committee
Juku: special private (cram) school attended after the regular school
　　day and at weekends
Jûkyo teate: housing allowance

Ka-chô: section chief
Kai-chô: chairman of the board of directors (*torishimari-yakkai*)
Kachô-hosa: deputy section chief
Kaigi: formal conference of managers usually held at some regular
　　interval
Kaisha-tsugô: company initiative, stands for involuntary separation
Kakari-chô: sub-section chief
Kami-sama: a god
Kanban: tag, usually in the context of Just-in-Time delivery
Kankei-gaisha: related companies
Kanri-sha: managers at the operational level
Kansa-yaku: statutory auditor
Keidanren: The Federation of Business Organizations
Keiei-sha: corporate executives
Kei-go: polite forms of the Japanese language
Keiretsu: 1) postwar industrial grouping; 2) distribution network
　　controlled by a major manufacturer
Keizai-Dôyûkai: Japan Association of Corporate Executives
Kengen: right to issue orders, authority, as opposed to influence
　　(*ken'i*)

Ken-i: influence arising from circumstances, as opposed to authority (*kengen*)
Ken-ri: rights
Kigyô-betsu kumiai: enterprise labour union (postwar)
Kihon-kyû: basic salary (monthly)
Kimatsu teate: seasonal allowance (in the public sector)
Kôhai: junior as opposed to senior (*sempai*)
Komon: advisor
Kondan-kai: informal meeting (here for decision-making)
Kyôdô-tai: community of fate

Matomari: pulling the threads together

Nemawashi: (gardener's term) laying the groundwork in decision-making
Nenkô: merit of years (of service)

Riji: substitute status title for upper *kanri-sha*
Ringi: often used for the Japanese decision-making process
Ringi-sho: document circulated in the context of *ringi*
Rôshi kyôgikai: joint labour–management council

Sanji: substitute status title for middle *kanri-sha*
Sempai: senior as opposed to junior (*kôhai*)
Semmu: executive managing director
Sha-chô: company president
Shachô-shô: company president's award
Sha-in: corporate member (colloquial for 'regular' employee)
Sha-in-kai: employee association
Shakai-jin: (adult) member of society (world of work)
Shingikai: deliberation board where bureaucrats, businessmen and experts meet
Shita-uke: subcontracting
Shitenchô-shô: branch head's award
Shitsu-chô: chief of office
Shoku-ba: workplace
Shoku-gyô: occupation, trade
Shokumu no kyû: grade (in government basic salary tables)
Shoku-taku: temporary employment
Shotei-nai kyûyo: scheduled cash earnings (monthly), excludes overtime pay
Shôyo: seasonal allowance (in the private sector)

Shûgyô kisoku: rules of employment; work rules
Shuji: see *shusa*
Shukkô: transfer, dispatch of personnel
Shunin: experienced clerk
Shuntô: Spring Wage Offensive staged by labour unions
Shusa: substitute status title for lower kanri-sha
Shûshin koyô: lifetime employment
Sôdan-yaku: advisor (board of directors)
Sôgô shôsha: general trading company
Sômu-bu: general affairs department (at corporate headquarters)

Taishoku-kin: separation allowance
Tansan: industry-wide federation of labour unions
Tatemae/honne: what is said versus what is thought
Teate: allowance (component of salary system)
Teinen: (mandatory) age limit
Torishimari-yakkai: (corporate) board of directors
Torishimari-yaku: (corporate) director
Tsûkin teate: commutation allowance

Uchi-awase: similar to 'working session' (here in decision-making)

Wa: harmony (relations among persons)
Wakon yôsai: Japanese spirit, Western techniques

Zaibatsu: prewar industrial group under a family-owned holding
   company

Index